AXEL VERVOORDT
LIVING WITH LIGHT

Text by Michael Gardner
Photography by Laziz Hamani

Flammarion

PAGE 1

This book takes readers
on a path to discover homes
around the globe, leading toward
the light. Different worlds meet
in a winding staircase designed
by French architect Jacques Couëlle
in curved white plaster, viewed
from behind stone walls—the
rough contrasts with the refined
as light descends from a skylight.
A nineteenth-century Chinese
root vase made in burr wood rests
atop a chestnut folding table
from Burgundy (c. 1700).

PAGES 2–3

At the home of Axel and May
Vervoordt in the castle of
s'Gravenwezel, the orangery was
transformed into a summer room
to enjoy the light shimmering
through the windows. Original white
lime walls were discovered underneath
layers of dirt. The sofa with fixed
pillows is by Axel Vervoordt Company.

PAGE 4

In a home on the Belgian seacoast
sits an early eighteenth-century
walnut console table, with an
earthenware bowl by Japanese
ceramist Shiro Tsujimura; on the
wall is an untitled 2009 work by
German artist Gotthard Graubner.

FACING PAGE

The elements of nature before
sunrise are seen from a picture
window in the breakfast kitchen
of a New England house, designed
by Cutler Anderson Architects.

Contents

Seeing is feeling with your eyes.
Jef Verheyen (1932–84)

"Lux est lex." *Light is law*. My close friend, the late Belgian painter Jef Verheyen, first uttered this sentence years ago, and it continues to have an important effect on my life and work today.

His words are authentic and true. Light is law. It is power, force, and life. Light is an energy that helps create the world and define our experiences. It informs every aspect of life and our unique way of living in this world.

Jef's paintings are deep meditations on the phenomena of light, landscape, and color. Through my experiences with his work and his passion for life, I learned to see the world differently. I discovered an openness for art that seeks to transcend time and space to reveal deeper meaning. I learned, in his words, to feel with my eyes.

In my life—and from a young age—I have always had the good fortune to count among my friends many artists. In addition to Jef, I've been lucky to have close friendships with philosophers, architects, gardeners, scientists, and musicians who have helped me to experience the world in new and interesting ways. Through their work, they have enabled me to understand and develop connections between the past, present, and future. It has been my goal in life to share this knowledge through my work, while developing a philosophy of living that seeks to embrace time and explore the nature of being.

We live at an increasingly fast pace in today's world. The way we live in our homes should offer balance and harmony. The space in which we share our private experiences with family and friends should not take energy, but restore and give energy. A home should not only be an escape from the outside world, but also an enlightening space that makes us happy. A house should reflect the personality and way of life of its owners. Our biggest aim is to ensure that people feel content in their homes, so that everyone who enters can also feel the happiness of life. Often, creating a home means searching for this emotion in every decision that's made.

PAGE 8
In s'Gravenwezel castle's cellar,
the 1978 work *Urbino—L'Espace
Ideal* (Urbino—Ideal Space) by
Belgian artist Jef Verheyen (1932–84)
finds the perfect light to display
its vibrations of color and energy.

LEFT
Axel created the Oriental drawing
room, which faces directly south, when
the family moved to the castle in 1986.
The philosophy of this space explores
the connections between East and
West, between architecture and nature,
between the past and the present.
It was the first room in which
Axel decided to mix the property's
earth with whitewash. He removed
the plaster ceiling and discovered
an original sixteenth-century beamed
ceiling. On the right wall is the 1972
Grand Marron Troué by Antoni Tàpies
(1923–2012). In the foreground,
a sandstone Buddha sculpture (Thailand,
pre-Angkorian Kingdom of Funan,
sixth–seventh century) watches the
light change. Next to the window
on the right, late Kamakura period
lion-dogs sit on an Artempo Interiorum
chest designed by Axel. Outside
in the park, created in the eighteenth
century, small trees are prepared
for years to bloom one day and share
their leaves and flowers with this room,
bringing nature's presence indoors.

When my wife May and I were in our early twenties, we started a small business and quickly developed a taste for objects with qualities that we felt were real, timeless, authentic, serene, and warm. Everything we chose to surround ourselves with created an extra dimension to our daily lives, as well as our way of thinking and seeing the world. I believe that the art of creating value is giving a better place to things. We are engaged in a process to help art, furniture, and objects find their true home. That's one reason why we could separate ourselves from objects we bought and loved very much—because we knew they could have a better place in the homes of our clients. Discovering things has always been the most important thing for me, and by giving some of those things a better home they always stay living in my mind.

Our taste corresponds to a philosophy—a way of life—rather than an expression of a certain style or fashion. This philosophy includes a quest for the universal spirit. Great art is timeless, and it's important to be surrounded by art and objects that not only reveal the essence of the time in which they were created, but also transcend time. Every project we are a part of aims to search for harmony and balance within art, architecture, and nature. I'm grateful to have a company that translates these ideas into everything we do.

From the early days of the company through today, May's work has been based on the pursuit of ephemerality, which is just as important as the eternal. Including the comfortable sofas, the textiles, the food, flowers, and candlelight, her work adds an extra dimension to the changing experiences of life. I'm very proud of the evolution and growth of my sons, Boris and Dick, and their achievements. Today, Dick concentrates on the redevelopment of historic building sites, and Boris takes a central role in the art gallery and interior design endeavors. As a family, we often enjoy a mutual understanding of taste even without words, and this is a very special experience. This energy extends to the many faithful and talented collaborators in our company who, in their quest for our philosophy, have found their own great voices and individual means of expression, as they create projects of their own. Their efforts and confidence have added a new dimension to our work, and allowed me to give more of my time and energy to explorations of art and philosophy, and to the organizing of exhibitions. Through art, I am able to have a better understanding of the evolution of time and to search for the profound meaning of the universal spirit. Knowledge of the past and the pursuit of the future enable us to act in the present to preserve our experiences.

I'm honored that we have been able to form lasting friendships with our clients, and I'm delighted to share this book with images of the work we have created together. As I look through these pictures, I'm reminded of the emotion inherent in vision. Seeing is feeling with the eyes. *Embrace the light.*

—Axel Vervoordt

FACING PAGE
In the home of a musician friend in Venice, a Korean vase rests atop an eighteenth–century French cabinet made of pine. The cabinet displays the markings of the passage of time, a reminder of Axel's idea of Artempo, where time produces art. Everything that an object experiences is like a performance embedded in the years and reflects its age.

PAGES 14–15
In a home in the south of France, light weaves its way through a linen curtain like fingers reaching into the darkness.

Light is not so much something that reveals,
as it is itself the revelation.
James Turrell (b. 1943)

Ever since my childhood, I've been fascinated with light, and in particular the dialogue between light and water. When I was eight years old, we took a family trip to Southeast Asia and I have a distinct memory of being mesmerized by the horizon during a particular sunset. The way the light danced on the water enchanted me. In the fading sunlight, there was an intensity of colors and shades that has left a powerful impression on me to this day. The sky was a brilliant canvas, made of shades of blue with endless subtleties of color. As we cultivate our awareness and attraction to certain shades, the perception of color is a sensibility that can change over time. This time, I had the sensation that I was not seeing color, but feeling it. I had an awareness of nature through all of my senses. I was spellbound. The smooth surface of the water had a sense of depth that was like a giant, mysterious void. Light reflected on the constantly changing surface of the water. It was a show created by nature and that evolved through time. The combinations were magical and extraordinary. The air was dense and warm. The scenery all around the horizon was composed of lush greens. I made a promise to myself—silently—to return one day to this part of the world and create a home for myself.

Life surprises us with its twists and turns, and some years later, I took a ride on a motorbike that changed the course of my life while—at the same time—bringing me back to the vision I had as an eight-year-old boy. Together with a friend, I fell in love with a property on the southeastern coast of Cambodia. It was a different country altogether than the one I'd visited on our family trip, and yet it was the start of a dream coming true. We were cruising without a map or a destination, so the discovery seemed at the time to be one of pure chance. The site consisted of three villas built in the 1960s by a pupil of Le Corbusier. Although the gardens were overgrown and the villas were empty and in dire need of restoration, when we rode past it was a revelation, and certainly love at first sight.

PAGE 16

An objet trouvé, this door was
brought to the former home of Pablo
Picasso with a respect for its condition,
as a work of art. Made from a single
plank of sixteenth-century chestnut
with its original patina, the door is
a symbol in this special home—a door
for humanity into a new world.
For Axel, it represents the philosophy
of two exhibitions he curated
at the Palazzo Fortuny in Venice:
Artempo: Where Time Becomes Art,
and TRA: The Edge of Becoming.

LEFT

In the historic center of Antwerp,
Belgium, a coffee-roasting factory
was transformed into the current
home of Boris Vervoordt and Michael
Gardner. Axel created the loft in
the early 1970s by removing part
of the ceiling and cutting an opening
into the chimney. The fireplace
is a source of warmth in the space,
conducive to conversation. To the left
is Michel Mouffe's 2012 *La Montagne
de L'Île*, and the sofa and armchair
are by the Axel Vervoordt Company.
To the right of the fireplace,
a 1962 Jef Verheyen painting hangs
near a 1960s slate table and a pair
of Chinese elm armchairs (Ch'ing
Dynasty, seventeenth century).
On the table is a wooden diamond,
a gift from friend Daniel de Belder.
On the balcony is a Chinese wooden
altar table (Ming Dynasty, 1368–1644)
with a collection of idols from
the Central Asian Margiana culture
(second millennium BCE).

The project began as a private guesthouse and later turned into a place that we wanted to share with more people. That's how it continues today, and although I'm no longer involved, the essence of the experience remains very close to me. This was the fulfillment of a personal promise that offered invaluable experiences, and was an expression of my passion for creating homes surrounded by nature. It was just one of many steps in a process that has continued with the projects in this book, developing a philosophy of how to create a home that is in pure harmony with the elements and its environment.

Our projects have brought us to many interesting locations, and we strive to think globally, while acting locally. It's a principle that we rely on every day and that can be accomplished through teamwork and a shared commitment of purpose. When nature and all of the elements are present in and around a home, every decision that's made concerning the way of life should strive for balance. Water, air, and light speak with a language that illuminates our existence in the world. We should endeavor not to speak against nature, but rather with nature.

When I was twenty-one years old, I made a commitment to my parents and started to work for the company. One of my first achievements with the team was developing the idea for the renovation project of the Kanaal—the industrial site that would become the new home for our offices. Today, the Kanaal is undergoing another transformation, led by my brother; we're creating new homes so that this special place for us can also be shared with others. Throughout my life, I've been very fortunate to learn from the creativity of my parents and the generosity of their spirit. Everything they do is about sharing, and I made the decision to be part of this environment they have created together.

Since the beginning of the company's activities, following the purchase of the Vlaeykensgang in Antwerp in 1968, the purpose has always been to search for harmony and comfort in the world of today, while building a future that respects the past; this is a central philosophy that continues in all of our activities. The Vlaeykensgang is a sixteenth-century pedestrian passage containing a series of houses, located next to Antwerp's City Hall and Great Market, in the shadow of an impressive cathedral constructed between 1352 and 1521. In the late 1960s, Axel began restoring the buildings and transformed them into a hidden collection of homes and restaurants. My partner and I feel very fortunate to have our home in the Vlaeykensgang and to be able to experience the unique, changing light in the city.

I'm keen to share the experiences my parents had throughout the restoration of the Vlaeykensgang, and also the emotions I felt during the work in s'Gravenwezel, Kanaal, and my ten years of client projects. These discoveries offer an explanation as to why we wanted to create this book and reveal the lessons I continue to learn in the course of my work.

FACING PAGE
Details of the home, clockwise from top left: a concrete and iron staircase designed by Axel Vervoordt in 1973; detail of an everyday object painted by Japanese artist Sadaharu Horio; an early nineteenth-century beech table in the kitchen was chosen for its strong and essential design, and an earthenware plate by Shiro Tsujimura sits in front of a window overlooking an outdoor corridor covered with wisteria; a 1962 matte lacquer-on-canvas work by Jef Verheyen hangs above a Chinese elm armchair (Ch'ing Dynasty, seventeenth century).

Pine flooring from a dressing room extends into the bathroom, as morning light streams in from two windows. Unique for its original painted canvas upholstery, the Pierre Jeanneret chair stands like a sculpture. Boris Vervoordt designed the bathroom with limestone and whitewash plastering, and the bathtub is by Devon & Devon.

It's important to listen to the ways that geography speaks to us. In our work, it's vital to analyze the necessity of the environment in which one chooses to live and to consider what the space can potentially bring to the family who will live there. As you read the stories of these residences, it will soon become apparent that you need to feel a special affinity with the place you choose to call home. People should love where they live, and home ought to be the happiest place on earth. One of the hardest lessons to learn is that if something is not there from the beginning, it will never be there. The location of a home is everything. It forms part of its narrative, and provides character and personality that contribute to the story of the people who live there.

Over the past twenty years, my responsibilities in the company have grown and I feel fortunate that my work involves doing what I love. It's a joy to be offered challenging work for inspiring clients who form lasting friendships with us. This passion extends to our teams, helping us all to grow.

Specifically, over the past several years I've been fascinated by the fact that we've helped create homes with a special connection to nature and the elements. Homes on the water or houses built next to the water with views of the horizon. There are historic homes in the country and modern homes in the city that share a curiosity for the past. Each project is unique, and yet what unites all of the images in this book is the fact that these are projects whose stories are told through the serenity and sensibility of light.

For me, these projects represent an encounter between intellectual enlightenment, spiritual enlightenment, and the physical and pure energy of natural light. My philosophy on living, from a young age through today, has been shaped by the idea that to live in an environment that's closely connected to nature brings peace. You can feel nature's illumination like a light in your brain. It cleanses your eyes and helps shape your spirit with its warm glow. The clarity gives you a sense of freedom. Through this freedom, you're more open to sharing experiences with all of those around you. In this state you're also more prepared to enter the world of artists, who through their work offer introspection and enlightenment. By choosing to live with art, you are choosing to be challenged and inspired through their acts of creation. I'm drawn to the idea of the contemporary *kunstkammer*—a classic art room—and the philosophy of living with artifacts from different cultures. Like light that expands across the horizon, art helps to broaden our consciousness and inspires us to live better lives.

From the beginning, art has been key to our work. Art elevates life and is crucial in helping us understand life. The notion of discovering what is essential is a primary influence in our interior philosophy. It's an endless search that drives our team every day.

RIGHT
An eighteenth-century staircase
and Pompeian red walls bring
the atmosphere of an old palazzo
to an apartment in Monaco.
On the wall is a rare Cycladic
marble figure. Some archaeologists
believe these idols express
supplication or prayer because
their faces look upward, or that
the figures are an idealized portrayal
of a Mother Goddess as a symbol
of fertility and rejuvenation.
The geometric, two-dimensional
form has a modern familiarity,
and the elegance and simple
lines of figures like this one
inspired artists including Brancusi,
Modigliani, and Picasso.

We seek materials that are authentic and possess noble qualities based on the simplicity and honesty of their origins. Our work often strives to understand dimensions in space, particularly the power and mystery of the void.

In every endeavor in life, it's important to remember that no one acts alone. I'm passionate about working as part of a team, and I'm thankful that the creation of these homes is the result of the collaboration of many people. The partnership with our team, architects, artists, designers, yacht builders, carpenters, painters, and everyone else who participates in all of the details has taught me a great deal. The relationship with them brings daily rewards. Their dedication and talent help to broaden the perspective of possibilities. We are an organization of strong individuals, and the leadership that our teams have shown at every step of each project is an inspiration. Together we strive to accomplish a balance between tradition and craft. We endeavor to create things that are well made. We work with people from around the world, and the lessons we learn from each other are necessary to understand how to build a new world that's ready for tomorrow.

This book is dedicated to those who created these dreams. To acknowledge their friendship and with the utmost respect for their vision, I dedicate *Axel Vervoordt: Living with Light* to the families who've allowed us to participate in the personal stories that are shared on the pages of this book. With tremendous gratitude and a lifetime of admiration, thank you.

This book is also dedicated to the everlasting memory and creative spirit of Lionel and Ibu (Iréna) Poilâne. As a young man, I was invited as a guest to their apartment in Paris and to their fort in Brittany. Visiting the fort was my first encounter with a home where the owners—through their love, care, and commitment to a vision—achieved a perfect balance of living in an environment surrounded by the elements of nature. The fort was built in the late eighteenth century; Lionel and Ibu made it their family home and in many ways they inhabited every corner of the island. They brought trees and stones, planted gardens, raised chickens, and thought of every detail. They embraced the elements of the fort's harsh architecture and approached them with great design and a creative vision of life. I have vivid memories of being in the kitchen with Lionel as he roasted bread on the fire and served it with honey produced on the island, or of walks on the beach with Ibu, when we would cut oysters from the rocks and drink vintage champagne. Ibu was one of the first people I encountered who introduced me to the beauty of twentieth-century architecture and design. Together, Lionel and Ibu inspired our family and me in countless ways. They took this timeless island and turned it into a treasure. We hope to honor their memory and original spirit by keeping these memories close, forever.

—Boris Vervoordt

FACING PAGE
In the headquarters of the Axel Vervoordt Company at Kanaal, along the Albert Canal just outside of Antwerp, the various elements of nature—the sky, light, and water—can be seen from almost every angle through the building's many windows over several floors. The Kanaal is a historic industrial site, and the walls are painted white to create a gallery feel and provide a blank canvas for the artworks. This room is dedicated to the artists represented by the Axel Vervoordt Gallery. Here, a 1999 work entitled *Regen* (Rain) by German artist Günther Uecker expresses the relations uniting water, man, and the power of nature to make the desert fertile. The Dutch Benedictine monk and architect Dom Hans van der Laan (1864–1942) designed the iron and wood monastery bench in the late 1950s for his Saint Benedict Abbey near Vaals.

PAGES 28–29
One of the inspirations for
the creation of this book is a fort
once owned by Lionel and Ibu Poilâne.
This is a view from the roof of the fort
over the beaches of Brittany as the
sun is setting. The island in front
is a natural reserve where thousands
of cormorants come to nest.

LEFT
As Boris says, "This is one of my
favorite kitchens in the world,
because of the wonderful meals
and moments that were created here
by the Poilâne family. I will never
forget the times we watched Lionel
roast bread on the fire. Or when
houseguests gathered around
on stools to share a wonderful glass
of wine from the cellar, as we
prepared to have a meal together.
These moments remain sacred in my
mind." In the eighteenth-century
building with a whitewashed ceiling,
Ibu and Lionel used marble, slate,
and African wood to create the kitchen,
making it warm and timeless.

A tribute to the legacy and memory of Lionel and Ibu Poilâne.

PAGES 34–35
For the main sitting room, Ibu and Lionel chose a pair of Venetian chandeliers
and three Axel Vervoordt sofas, which are placed in front of the room's two
fireplaces (one of which is pictured here). Ibu designed a pair of deck chairs in teak
and linen and the Axel Vervoordt Company created the chestnut coffee table.

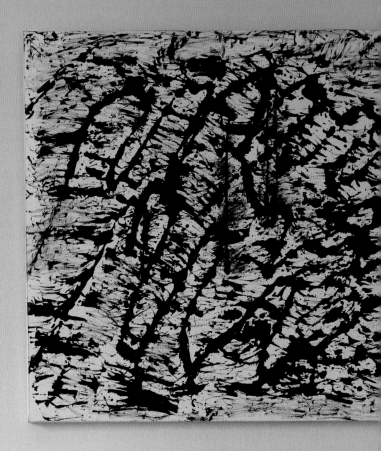

When a man is tired of London, he is tired of life;
for there is in London all that life can afford.
Samuel Johnson (1709–84)

London is an ancient city whose history stretches back to its founding over two thousand years ago and whose present ambitions seem to stretch by a similar measure at least that far into the future. Rooted in time, the city's iconic landmarks represent the core of its soul. Their ambition is awe-inspiring and expressed through the power of art and architecture as they strive for a complex harmony between timelessness and tradition. London is a thoroughly modern city as well, and even its contradictions possess a certain kind of style. It's one of the world's greatest cities because of its endlessly interesting features, and perhaps its greatest asset is that it yearns to be explored. To live in London is to share a fascination with the past, honoring the city's remarkable history while building one's own future. The themes of exploration and curiosity are the basis of the interior concepts for an apartment in a bustling center of London. The owners wanted a true city home—an intellectual space that blends its public setting with a private philosophy of entertaining surrounded by close family and friends. Overcoming the challenging economies of living space that are characteristic of many cities of this size, the apartment was conceived as a *kunstkammer*—a classic art room—where the family's collection of artifacts and art offers daily inspiration and invites reflection. Furniture—ranging from the eighteenth to twentieth centuries—was chosen for its intrinsic sculptural qualities. Figures and objects from all over the world create a composition on the mantel that spans centuries and civilizations. A painting by the late Catalan artist Antoni Tàpies, an Irish hunt table, and a chair by Pierre Jeanneret come together like participants in an exhilarating conversation. In London, sunlight can be scarce, so in this home light has an important metaphorical representation through enlightenment. Many elements pay homage to Sir John Soane (1753–1837), the great English neoclassical architect and collector whose London home is now a museum. Soane's careful presentation of his collection along with his eye for clean details, exceptional lines, skillful proportions, and a masterful use of light influenced the design philosophy achieved here. Like the Grand Tours of Europe taken from London three hundred years ago, the home exemplifies a passionate curiosity for art, culture, and civilization. In a historic city that aims to share experiences and knowledge with the future, this is a home that artfully knows its place.

PAGE 36

In a space that serves as both an office and a guest room, the assembled artworks explore the freedom of the sketch and the gesture of the creative act. Above the sofa and the Postman DKW leather chair by Charles and Ray Eames are a small painting by German artist Raimund Girke (1930–2002), a painting by Belgian-born French artist and writer Henri Michaux (1899–1984), and a drawing by Belgian artist Antoine Mortier (1908–99).

RIGHT

The view of the dining room and adjoining sitting room encompasses art, furniture, and objects that span centuries and civilizations. In the foreground is an eighteenth-century Irish table. Above the Steinway upright piano is a 1969 aluminum relief by German artist Heinz Mack that both captures and releases the light. In the background is an English Regency klismos chair (c. 1811–20) and to the right of the fireplace is an Aboriginal churinga, or sacred board made of wood. Farther right, on the library shelves is an original 1961 *Superficie Magnetica* installation by Italian artist and designer Davide Boriani. In the foreground, on the right wall is a dripping painting titled *Line* by Russian-Ukranian artist Evgeny Mikhnov-Voitenko (1932–88).

PAGE 40

A terra-cotta cuneiform tablet from Mesopotamia (c. 2028 BCE). Cuneiform script was one of the world's earliest forms of writing.

PAGE 41

Above the fireplace is a mixed media work on canvas by Catalan painter and sculptor Antoni Tàpies titled *Grey of the Vertical Cross* (1960). The composition of figures on the mantel spans continents and includes (from left to right): a large, eighteenth-century Timor mask with angular features, which was ritually placed in the doorway of a house to protect its inhabitants; a stone figurine from the Valdivia culture (Ecuador, second millennium BCE); an anthropomorphic rectangular stele in alabaster (Yemen, Sabaean Kingdom, first century BCE–first century CE), a type of funerary figure; the 1963 sculpture *Figure of the Wood* by Hans Arp (also known as Jean Arp).

PAGE 42

A corner of the sitting room warmed
by soft daylight includes a work
by German artist Gotthard Graubner,
Stilles Leuchten II (Silent Glow).
For Graubner, color is the medium
through which his work expresses
itself and his three-dimensional cushion
paintings transform the perception
of color through volume and space.
On top of an English Regency table
(c. 1815) made in mahogany and
leather is a nineteenth-century Chinese
porcelain vase selected for its simplicity
and elegance, and a 1960 bronze
reading lamp from France. The chair
and sofa are Axel Vervoordt creations.

PAGE 43

A detail of a pedestal partners desk
(also called a double desk) in satin birch
from Victorian England and a 1951
Postman DKW leather and wood chair
by Charles and Ray Eames.

RIGHT

A conversational space for creating
memories with food, family, and
friends, the dining room includes
an eighteenth-century Irish table
in mahogany and a 1964 work by Antoni
Tàpies titled *Materia Sobre Lienzo
y Papel Collage*. The mixed-media work
is an evocation of memory and a spiritual
reflection of the nature of humanity.
On the right is an eighteenth-century
walnut secretary and bookcase from
Ireland, holding a desk lamp (c. 1930)
attributed to French architect and
designer René Herbst (1891–1982)
and a celadon vase from Korea (early
Yin Dynasty, fourteenth century).
The chairs include a George III English
wing chair in mahogany (c. 1775),
an early eighteenth-century English
library armchair in walnut, and
a Senate armchair by Pierre Jeanneret
in teak (c. 1960).

PAGE 46

This is a home that blends character with intelligence, and in the bathroom the John Soane inspiration becomes more literal. As the view from this space is not a clear one due to the opaque window, it was important to add a refreshing sense of awakening through the objects. On the far wall is a pair of tripodal bronze vases (Gallo-Roman period, first–second century), a white marble commemorative plaque (Roman, second–third century), and a fragment of a Satyr's head in white marble (Roman, second century). On the near wall is a circular French sorceress mirror (c. 1900). According to legend, only the reflection of a sorceress would not be distorted by these mysterious convex mirrors. On the counter is the white marble head of a herm, a sacred stone object connected to the cult of Hermes, the messenger god (Roman, first–second century).

PAGE 47

A fragment of a labrum sculpted in bas-relief with the scene of a lion attacking a deer (Roman, third century). A labrum was a large, water-filled basin, which was often incorporated in the architecture of Roman bath complexes.

FACING PAGE

Details of the home (from left to right): a charming view into a child's bedroom; the head of a sphinx in sandstone (Egyptian, Ptolemaic period, 332–30 BCE); a miniature painting created in 1961 by Japanese Gutai artist Kazuo Shiraga; a Senate armchair by Pierre Jeanneret (c. 1960); light and the shadow of a lamp on the surface of a walnut desk designed for the space; an English iron and leather X-frame campaign stool (c. 1890); a side view of Gotthard Graubner's 2010 *Stilles Leuchten II* (Silent Glow); a sandstone torso of Bodhisattva Avalokiteshvara from Thailand (pre-Angkorian period, seventh–eighth century)—since there are no gods in Buddhism, male and female bodhisattvas, or enlightened beings, are often depicted in sculpture; and finally, the hallway corridor with a mirrored cabinet and a half-relief Egyptian tablet representing Isis on the throne (c. third century BCE).

PAGE 50

The master bedroom furnishings include an English X-frame leather and wood campaign stool (c. 1890) at the foot of the bed and an English walnut lowboy with three drawers (c. 1720) as a bedside table. A sandstone torso of Bodhisattva Avalokiteshvara from Thailand presides along the wall.

PAGE 51

Carte de Voyage (*Detail: 2323817-2325573*) by Roman Opalka (1931–2011). In 1965, Opalka began his series of counted paintings, from one to infinity, a lifelong work of painting numbers in sequence starting from the number one. Each painting is the same size, and on each one the numbers are painted in white, in even rows from one edge to the other. Since Opalka didn't want to interrupt his work while he was traveling from his home in France to his native Poland—where he was viewed as a dissident—he created a *carte de voyage*, a piece of paper on which he wrote the numbers in ink. As he said, "All my work is a single thing, the description from number one to infinity. A single thing, a single life."

... I am merely a man making signs in the sand.
I made these holes. But what are they?
They are the mystery of the Unknown in art,
they are the Expectation of something that must follow.
Lucio Fontana (1899–1968)

Born in Argentina, the Italian artist, painter, and sculptor Lucio Fontana realized it was the nature of light that captured and captivated man's imagination. His slashed canvases with a seemingly infinite space at the center are like portals into the void. Pregnant with possibility, the cuts are openings into new dimensions that absorb light and seek to explore the universe and its infinite reach. The rhythm and the expressiveness of these holes are mystifying. When one appreciates an artist like Fontana while admiring the sweeping sea views that span the horizon at a coastal retreat in Belgium, the slashes seem expansive and endless. In this area, an entrepreneur desired to make a home for himself. The views are symbolic—he is a sea trader and the content of the horizon connects him to the origins of his business. In a multi-family building, Axel's goal was to create a home that speaks in a contemporary language by deleting all superfluous decoration. The aim was to respect the rules of great architecture: noble proportions and honesty of materials. The materials used here are few. Giving the thresholds a sense of strength, door surrounds are made of the same stone used in the kitchen and bathrooms. The walls are whitewashed, reminiscent of the sand from the beach only a stone's throw away. Partitions and doors are walnut, and floors are oak. Most remarkably, every floor plank goes wall to wall, and some are as long as forty-three feet (thirteen meters). Light has space to dance. These are natural materials that age beautifully. In order to create volume, furniture was chosen for its intrinsic qualities. A very rare and unrestored fifteenth-century Flemish chest is a superb example of Artempo—the idea that time can turn some objects into works of art. There is purity in the presence of the objects in this home. The art collection includes works by Piero Manzoni, Lucio Fontana, Günther Uecker, Dominique Stroobant, Serge Poliakoff, and Kazuo Shiraga—gesture artists whose work with space, nails, stone, and paint help break through the surface of man's understanding of form, color, space, and light. With its background palette of subtle shades of green thanks to the luxuriant nature, and the sand and sea in front, this home is a testament to art that is an artwork in itself.

PAGE 52

The extended, three-room view
includes a 1941 Primavera day bed
in the foreground, made of wood
and leather by the Mexico-based
design team Michael Van Beuren,
Klaus Grabe, and Morley Webb.
On the wall, the energy of the artistic
process is palpable in a 1981 work
by German artist Günther Uecker
titled *Interferenzen* (Interferences).
In the far background, a painting
by Russian-born French artist
Serge Poliakoff (1906–69) hangs
in the bedroom.

RIGHT

The central sitting room is anchored
by the owner's art collection,
featuring works by Günther Uecker
and Italian artist Lucio Fontana
(1869–1968), as well as a collection
of furniture and objects. On the left
wall, Fontana's 1960 *Concetto
Spaziale, Attese* refers to space,
infinity, and the void out of which
everything is born, just like the sea
outside. In front of the three terrace
windows is a work in black granite
titled *Ascia H8* by Belgian artist
Dominique Stroobant. Behind
the sofa, on a seventeenth-century
French table, is a trio of triangulated,
pre-Columbian Zemi stones
(1000–1500) from the Caribbean.
At right is a fifteenth-century oak
chest from Flanders.

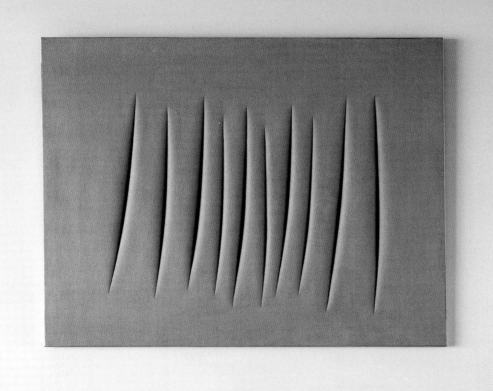

PAGES 56–57
In the central sitting room, Lucio Fontana's *Concetto Spaziale, Attese* is presented with a full view (p. 56) and a close detail view (p. 57). The translation of the title is Spatial Concept, At Peace, and the work represents the peace that comes from the void, exposed by the artist's innovative slashes. The Fontana hangs above a fifteenth-century Gothic chest from Flanders, made of strong oak panels, with rudimentary animal claws at the base that elegantly contrast with medieval ironwork using a fleur-de-lis motif.

LEFT
On the right wall is an ancient cuneiform tablet (878–859 BCE) describing the rule of Ashurnasirpal II, King of Assyria. On the left is a 1961 painting by Kazuo Shiraga (1924–2008), one of the founding members of Gutai, a Japanese post-WWII art movement. Shiraga was an action painter who placed paint on the canvas and spread it violently with his body and feet.

PAGES 60–61

Detail of a door handle made from horn, designed for the home by
Axel Vervoordt. The door is bleached walnut; the door and floor surrounds
are made of Buxy limestone. Four solid stones were used for each doorway,
including the frames and the threshold. The oak floorboards extend from wall
to wall. A 1958 *Achrome* by Italian artist Piero Manzoni hangs in the hallway
in dialogue with the two works by Lucio Fontana on the opposite wall.

FACING PAGE

Light streams into the kitchen. The floor, countertops, and back wall are
made of Buxy limestone. The shelving and drawers are custom-made in walnut
and the stove is from La Cornue. A collection of French Vallauris pottery
is on the shelves and the wooden serving trays are from Axel Vervoordt.

LEFT
The terrace overlooks a sweeping terrain of dunes and a nature reserve. The light and landscape offer inspiration from the early morning to the late evening. The furniture includes a table and chairs made by Axel Vervoordt.

PAGE 66
The themes of light and texture define the serene bedroom with objects selected for their primitiveness and the mystery of their origins. On the left is an Artempo bedside table cube created by Axel Vervoordt, called Setting Moon. Lucio Fontana's *Concetto Spaziale, Attese* (1964) hangs above the bed.

PAGE 67
An antique French table in pine with a warm patina is placed next to the window, with an Italian Bellino armchair typical of the montagnard (or mountain dweller) style. On the table is a vase with a natural ash glaze by Shiro Tsujimura, a potter who produces works following traditional Japanese methods from the fifteenth and sixteenth centuries, such as Shigaraki.

Whatever good things we build end up building us.
Jim Rohn (1930–2009)

During the seventeenth and eighteenth centuries, life in Europe was in a remarkable state of transition and change. The origins of today's modernity are often examined through the lens of the intellectual, political, and social movements during this Age of Enlightenment. Nearly every field of study produced new ideas that dominated the cultural landscape and shaped collective thoughts with far-reaching consequences. Also known as the Age of Reason, this time period represented significant changes in the ways that man viewed himself, the pursuit of knowledge, laws, and the universe at large. Important figures produced new ideas in nearly every field of study. Science and skepticism reigned. The era might also have been called the age of philosophy, nature, education, exploration, progress, and the arts. Individuals—dreaming of freedom and a brighter age—felt exhilarated by intelligence, knowledge, and the power of ideas. Evidence of man trying to make meaning of the world is evident in the work of philosophers such as the French rationalist and mathematician René Descartes, who studied the theory and properties of light. It's this combination of enlightenment and light that one senses in a very deep way when visiting an eighteenth-century château in the Belgian countryside. The property is a bridge through history, and the home is a genuine reflection of its time. Through a meticulous renovation process, Axel Vervoordt's goal was to help tell the story of the home while making it livable and interesting—a family space filled with warmth and comfort. In a historical house, every addition tells a new story and the point is not to add anything that changes the narrative. Every addition must be authentic and able to stand the test of time. Original floors, staircases, moldings, and doors were enlivened by the rich period details of European furniture from Belgium, France, Italy, and England. Restorations included a pool, which was built within existing side buildings, and a carriage house was transformed into a "feast" room to offer an inviting space for receiving numerous guests. A main drawing room includes Belgian impressionist art and comfortable chairs and sofas, while the amber color palette of the walls complements the soft natural light and poetic garden views. Jacques Wirtz designed the garden, one of his latest great masterpieces. A gentleman's study showcases a French architectural library, with a collection of scientific objects, along with a painting by Marc Chagall. There are inspiring spaces for entertaining, thinking, reflecting, and living. Axel says the joy in creating a home comes from discovery—the creative process of finding furniture and objects that belong to a home and feel as if they've always been there. This is a warm, family home that elegantly connects the past and present with timeless style.

PAGE 68

The grand party room is used
for entertaining large groups
of guests—during the day, when
sunlight streams through the
tall windows, and at night, with
candlelight providing festive
illumination. A monumental
Italian credenza made in walnut
(c. 1660), originally used in
a church sacristy, anchors the
room. A trio of eighteenth-century
Italian chestnut chandeliers
is hung with pulleys to raise
and lower the candlelight.
A seventeenth-century painting
titled *Smell*, one of a series called
The Five Senses attributed
to Abraham Janssen, hangs on
the inner wall. Furnishings include
a pair of Louis XIII armchairs
and an English oak table.

RIGHT

One of Belgian landscape
designer Jacques Wirtz's latest
masterpieces, the park with
its sweeping views demonstrates
the transformation of an
eighteenth-century design that
has been redeveloped with
a contemporary vision of landscape
architecture. It's a harmonious
balance between past and present.
The exterior view of the castle
shows the home's many windows,
which serve as a reference
to the period of its creation,
during the "century of light."

PAGE 72

The view from an entrance hall extends through the main sitting room to the blue sky and lush greenery in the back garden. Atop the original black-and-white marble flooring in the foreground is an unusually large, round mahogany table with a pure, harmonious form (c. 1830) by Gillows of Lancaster. On the table is a French silvered centerpiece with four candleholders (c. 1720). The doorway is framed by a pair of iron vases placed on two eighteenth-century French console tables made in walnut with blue Turquin marble tops, and a Baroque Flemish hall lantern hangs overhead.

PAGE 73

An original eighteenth-century staircase swirls through the home, connecting its layered stories.

RIGHT

The soft, warm, and elegant color palette in the central drawing room complements the poetic garden views and a collection of Belgian impressionist paintings by artists of the Latem School (named after the small town of Sint-Martens-Latem in East Flanders where they worked). In the foreground is a large George II console table in bleached mahogany and marble, with a pair of seventeenth-century silver *tazze*, or serving dishes. Hanging overhead is a 1795 chandelier made of Bohemian crystal, prized for its weight, clarity, and hardness. In the background is a set of four Louis XV armchairs by Louis Delanois and, on the windowsill, a small bronze *Danseuse* (Dancer) by Edgar Degas, cast from an original created in the late nineteenth century.

PAGE 76
Above one of a pair of Italian
seventeenth-century walnut settees
is one of two 1970 paintings by
Jef Verheyen, who was born with
a severe ophthalmological handicap
and painted light to bring light into
his life and to escape from darkness.
Color represents nothing but color,
and for him emptiness is the place
where essence is revealed.

PAGE 77
In the warm family kitchen
is an eighteenth-century Italian
chestnut table as well as a walnut
sideboard with drawers (c. 1740)
that was originally part of the
sacristy in a Huguenot chapel
in Lyon. Above it hangs a domestic
interior painted by Flemish
artist Léon De Smet (1881–1966).
The seventeenth-century German
copper chandelier has twelve arms
and is adorned with an eagle motif.

LEFT
Bathed in light through brilliant
picture windows, the large
walnut cabinets that surround
the kitchen were originally part
of a nineteenth-century French
pharmacy. La Cornue built the kitchen
island. Both the countertops and
flooring are made of Verona marble.

LEFT
An architectural, neoclassic French library wall in mahogany from the early nineteenth century houses the owners' collection of scientific astronomical instruments. Atop the eighteenth-century English desk is a neoclassic Greek urn-shaped vase lamp in green porphyry and a bronze torso of the Greek hero Heracles (the Roman Hercules) from the Hellenistic period (fourth–first century BCE) that powerfully captures the balance between tension and relaxation. Overhead is an early nineteenth-century crystal and copper French chandelier. Above the marble mantelpiece, *L'Âne Rouge* by Marc Chagall (1958–59) presides over the room.

PAGES 82–83
A serene atmosphere exists in the attic, which serves as an entertaining
space for family and friends as well as a place for quiet relaxation. Across the
room from a collection of Axel Vervoordt furniture, a leather bench doubles
as a concealed storage space for a movable home cinema projector and screen.
Beneath the exposed original roof beams are rustic floors made of reclaimed oak.

FACING PAGE
Details from the home (clockwise from top left): a long corridor near the pool
creates arches of light in one of the home's side buildings. Built in collaboration
with Belgian architect Stephane Boens, the space was transformed into an
inspiring oasis of tranquil recreation; a marble Roman statue of a *togatus* (a male
wearing a draped toga) from the second century, placed beside the pool; windows
of the pool room reflected in the water; at the opposite end of the pool, a Roman
marble portrait of a lady (first–second century CE) copied from a Greek original.

PAGES 86–87
The reflective surface of the water mirrors the exposed ceiling as well
as the brilliant light. In a timeless dialogue with the environment, the marble
Roman lady is standing with her weight on her left leg, and she wears
a long himation draped as a veil, falling in long folds down by her side.

Art is a harmony parallel with nature.
Paul Cézanne (1839–1906)

The clear air and crystalline light in the southeast region of France has been seducing residents and visitors for thousands of years. The allure was strong enough to entice the Romans across the Alps to create their first province beyond Italy. The ruins in southern France are a testament to their architectural achievements, and to their adoration of the landscape and the light so specific to the region. Steeped in romance and rooted in history, the Provençal light actually has scientific explanations. The harsh, powerful mistral winds sweep down the Rhône Valley, blowing away dust and atmospheric debris, leaving in their wake clear skies and the warm, glowing, golden sun. Here, the balance of beauty is truly created by the blowing wind. The intensities and subtleties of color are unlocked by the clarity of light, offering rich hues to the painter's palette and inspiration for the writer's pen. In this land where thick vines and groves of olive trees grow, a European family fell in love with the energy of the area and its distinctive sensations of light. The origins of their home date to the end of the eighteenth century, when a château was added next to a *mas*, or traditional farmhouse, that had been built as the annex to an olive press. Today, in the surrounding gardens, the music of the locusts and of the flowing water from original fountains pays tribute to the home's history. Through a close collaboration with the family, based on a longtime friendship, Axel and Boris partnered with Pierre-Olivier Brèche Architects as well as the owners to create inspiring living spaces and restore the property to its natural greatness. The quality of light throughout the house adds to the visual sensations of the family's collection of modern and contemporary art and sculpture, including works by Renoir, Enrico Castellani, Markus Raetz, and Anish Kapoor. Objects are bathed in light. These artworks share space with French and Italian furniture that is full of personality. Marble fireplaces, terra-cotta tiles, and limestone flooring were chosen for their character and color. Light and the emotions of nature inspired all of the decisions in this country paradise. Blending casual formality with a sense of relaxed elegance, this home is an enduring expression of the intelligent pleasures of life and the pure lightness of being.

PAGE 88

A view of the hallway reveals a marble
sculpture by Indian-born British
sculptor Anish Kapoor (Untitled, 2002)
as a welcoming gesture into the void.
As Kapoor explains it himself, "This very
physically monolithic object then appears
to create within itself an ephemeral
reflection akin to an ethereal flame."

PAGE 90

The view of an original staircase
uncovers the home's hidden layers.
Here, a window from a previous facade
became a passage to a new library
space. The installation of wooden
books is a 1979 work by Herman de Vries
titled *Die Bücher*.

PAGE 91

Above an eighteenth-century
French chest of drawers in walnut
is a print by American artist Ellsworth
Kelly. With a pure, minimalist aesthetic,
a trio of late nineteenth- to early
twentieth-century white porcelain
vases from Korea present flowers from
the property's gardens.

RIGHT

A succession of rooms was combined
to create one main drawing room
that captures the home's guiding
philosophies of living with light and art.
The seventeenth-century Palladian
fireplace surround is marble, and the floor
is *cocciopesto*, made of crushed marble,
terra-cotta, and lime mortar. The mix
of French and Italian furniture includes
a Louis XV walnut library table.
From left to right, the artworks include
a sculpture by William Turnbull (*Head 3*,
1993); a bronze sculpture by Joel Shapiro
(Untitled, 2001); an untitled work by
Markus Raetz; an aluminum and ebonite
lamp by Jacques Le Chevallier and René
Koechlin (Lampe à pans mobile n°40,
c. 1928); a sculpture by A.R. Penck
(Untitled, 1977), and, against the wall,
is a monumental head of a herm, a sacred
object in white marble connected
to the cult of Hermes, the messenger god
(Roman, first–second century CE).

PAGE 94

Beyond the steps, the view
extends toward the dining room.
This warm and quiet room is
situated in the seventeenth-century
part of the house and includes an
eighteenth-century French chair,
which sits next to the original fireplace.
A collection of candlesticks sits atop
the mantel with eighteenth-century
French fire irons below.

PAGE 95

This space was the castle's original
kitchen and is now used as a flower
room. The furniture and objects
include an early eighteenth-century
French *Os de Mouton* armchair
and a seventeenth-century table
with a slate top. On the mantel
is a collection of ceramic duck nests.

LEFT

An interesting, playful detail
in this festive dining room is the
white plaster motifs above each door
depicting the four seasons. However,
since there are only three doors
in the space, the season of winter
is missing. This is a welcome oversight
in a summer home. A relief painting
by Italian artist Enrico Castellani
presides over the room (Untitled,
1967) next to an eighteenth-century
Aix-en-Provence chest of drawers
in walnut with a marble top and
Maltese crosses on the doors.
On top is a collection of glass vases
and objects. Above the table hangs
an eighteenth-century Piedmont
crystal chandelier. On the table are
French silvered-metal candelabras.
Around the table and elsewhere
in the room is a series of Louis XVI
Italian armchairs. Completing the
space are four French Empire marble
vases (1804–15).

PAGE 98

Light and shadow merge across a detail of an untitled 1967 work by Enrico Castellani. The influential Italian artist works up his canvases with nails and a nail gun to give the surface a uniform relief texture that produces effects of light and shape through indentations and protrusions, altering the perception of space altogether.

PAGE 99

The play of light and shadow on a bronze cast sculpture by French impressionist artist Pierre-Auguste Renoir, which was a study for the statue of Venus Victrix, created with the help of sculptor Richard Guino.

FACING PAGE

A long view of the library leads to the central drawing room, forming a pathway of learning; it holds monographic books on artists, gardening, and other subjects that interest the family. The bronze figures are seventeenth-century slaves attributed to Italian sculptor Pietro Tacca (1577–1640). In this space, the mixture of French and Italian furniture includes a French bergère and a pair of eighteenth-century walnut stools with their original leather.

PAGE 102

An intimate detail of one of a series of six Louis XV armchairs by Jean-Baptiste Le Rouge, made in beech with their original embroidery. The precise proportions and curves are characteristic of the rules of the 1750s. Axel Vervoordt restored the chairs with his signature Interiorum philosophy by turning the colorful embroidery inside out to reveal the hidden side. As he states, "Its time-determined and yet ageless soul becomes the outside, visible to the world in all its beauty."

PAGE 103

A mobile work by Swiss artist Markus Raetz titled *Doppelpaar* (2009–10) hangs above the Nine table made of limestone, designed by Vervoordt.

PAGES 104–5

Inspired by art and nature, the color palette in one of the guest bedrooms is achieved with an indigo pigment that was used for painting the walls. Displayed on the wall is a 1985 oil-on-canvas painting by Austrian artist Herbert Brandl titled *Weidenmulde*. A nineteenth-century blue ceramic pot from the Languedoc region rests atop an eighteenth-century French chest of drawers with original red paint. In front of the light-filled window is an eighteenth-century French armchair covered in antique linen.

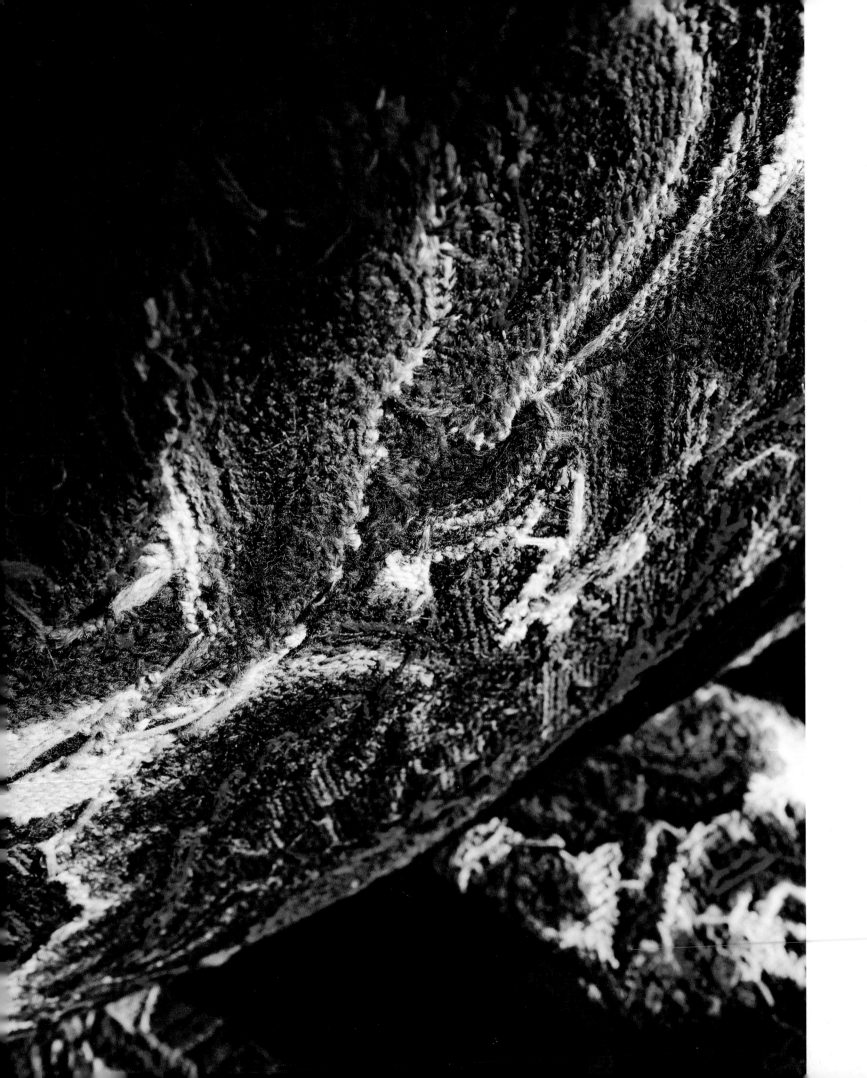

Invention combines history with images.

Giorgio Vasari, 1550

Nature's purity, power, and surprising language define the experience of life along a uniquely private stretch of coastline on the Italian side of the Mediterranean Sea. Backed by steep hills in a mountainous landscape, a humble road with Roman origins carves a very narrow path to a sixteenth-century home next to the water, surrounded by poetic vegetable gardens, and olive and citrus trees. Traveling the road, one already feels a sense of creative transformation—it's a path guided through time. The home was originally built as a monastery and many elements were added in different times and in different styles. Upon analysis, the additions were kept if they respected the architecture, proportions, and volumes of the space and if they were an honest expression of their own time. Axel Vervoordt restored the house in the hope of retaining a sense of its original serenity by creating living spaces inspired by warm, enlightened minimalism. The purpose was to find harmony between monastic architecture—in which the only decoration is proportion—and the lyrical charm of country life. A further aim was to balance the Renaissance spirit of palace life with the cosmic connection of the sea's force pounding the rocks outside. In the process of the restoration, the study of sacred proportions helped uncover the original floor plan. By shifting a wall and a staircase, the house seemed to find space to breathe and a sense of harmony was achieved. Original arches and dome ceilings from the sixteenth century were saved and essential details added. Special discoveries seemed destined for this environment, including a painted polychrome ceiling and floors made of eighteenth-century white Carrara marble and terra-cotta tiles. There is a large slate table made in the Vervoordt's Belgian workshops, along with pure seventeenth-century Italian furniture in its original condition, patinated like abstract art. Tables made of eighteenth-century pine from an Italian monastery travel throughout the house—indoors and out—for entertaining by day as well as special occasions under the moonlight. Old walnut doors were chosen for their authenticity of texture in the spirit of Artempo, in which time creates art. This home peacefully combines the coziness of a kitchen and the warmth of a drawing room with a sense of serenity and spirituality. The owners are passionate collectors of Renaissance and contemporary art, as well as devoted music lovers. Axel created a special room for them called a *puits de lumière*, or well of light, an underground inner space filled with natural light from a skylight above. Based on the sacred proportion of four times the perfect cube, the room is used for concerts, exhibitions, or kept totally empty, like a temple for the light. When you walk outside, the wild sea confronts you as it crashes onto huge rocks. This is an inspirational, inventive home that travels through the past and present, and looks to the future as it seeks to feel the timeless energy of nature, architecture, and art. Like landscape paintings, the views give the impression that one is standing on the bow of a great ship at rest.

PAGE 106
Like a timeless landscape painting, a bay window frames the view and brings
nature into the picture gallery. On the left is the exquisite *Portrait of a Man*
by Milanese artist Bernardino dei Conti, a favorite disciple of Leonardo da Vinci.
On the right, the serene and exalted portrait of Duke Cosimo I dei Medici (c. 1545)
by master mannerist painter Agnolo Bronzino (Il Bronzino, 1503–72) reigns
over the room. Light graces the surface of the seventeenth-century Italian polychrome
ceiling of the room, for which Axel Vervoordt created a coffee table using an
eighteenth-century Brèche marble top. In the corner of the room is a French armchair
à crémaillères (with a system that reclines the back) with its original footstool.

FACING PAGE
Rather than install a typical balustrade in between the stone walls as a protective railing
along the sea, Axel Vervoordt created a steel sculpture which serves the same purpose,
while artfully framing the sky, sea views, and horizon line like a window onto the void.

PAGES 110–11

Based on the sacred proportion of four times the perfect cube, an underground
inner space of light called a *puits de lumière* (well of light) was created.
This versatile space is used for concerts, exhibitions, and other events organized
by the family, or kept totally empty as a temple for the light. Designed specifically
for the project, a pair of sliding metal doors encloses the space as the corridor
leads toward the immense stone walls and sea views outside.

FACING PAGE

An exposed wooden ceiling leads toward a skylight that naturally illuminates
a small wooden stage, like a Japanese *tokonoma*—an alcove reserved for art and
flowers. In a home that blends the power of nature, architecture, and art,
this space captures the pure and peaceful energy of the philosophy of life here.

RIGHT

This refined gallery sitting room
is perfect for enjoying the expansive
views. The furniture includes an
eighteenth-century Italian refectory
table in pine surrounded by a series of
six seventeenth-century Italian chairs
with *point de Hongrie* upholstery,
protected by slipcovers. The rest
of the furnishings are creations by
the Axel Vervoordt Company.

PAGE 116

The perspective through the doorway
from the warm sitting room shows
another view of the Italian refectory
table in the adjoining space.
On the wall is a magical painting,
Mother and Child by Sienese painter
Sano di Pietro (1405–81). On the right
is a sixteenth-century architectural
cabinet from the Loire Valley in France,
decorated with mother of pearl
and ivory inlaid work *à la royale*.

PAGE 117

This room connects the picture
gallery and dining room. The long
view shows two works by master
Italian mannerists in dialogue.
Agnolo Bronzino's portrait of Duke
Cosimo I dei Medici is in the
background at the top of the stairs,
and on the right wall is a portrait
by Jacopo da Pontormo (1494–1557).
Another of the most significant
painters in Florence, Pontormo had
an important influence on Bronzino's
work, and his style can be distinguished
by a highly original iconography
and composition.

LEFT
The warm family kitchen is the heart of the home, connecting its inner layers with the pathways to the surrounding gardens. The kitchen cabinetry is made from eighteenth-century Italian walnut, with slate countertops. The problem of the large refrigerator was solved by covering it like a blackboard, allowing the playful expression of the family's artistic influences. The flooring is white Carrara marble and black Belgian marble. The long slate table in the background was made by the Axel Vervoordt Company.

PAGE 120
Light pours in from the surrounding landscape onto the long slate table in the dining gallery. Around the table the mixed seating includes six Louis XIV chairs protected by linen slipcovers. Overhead, a pair of French chandeliers (c. 1800) hangs from the home's original arched ceilings. A decision was made to cover the walls in white Delft tiles, a style that was also used in Italy in the late eighteenth century.

PAGE 121
In a home filled with light, shadows cast on white walls are transformed into paintings.

PAGES 122–23
The ageless sea provides an endless canvas in dialogue with the sky and the changing elements of nature.

We shape our buildings. Thereafter, they shape us.
Winston Churchill (1874–1965)

Brussels is a modern capital whose beginnings can be traced to a fortress built on a river island toward the end of the tenth century. Today, it's a cosmopolitan city of more than one million residents that sits proudly in the heart of Western Europe. A majority of its citizens come from elsewhere, and it's precisely this rich, diverse ethnic mix that gives this large Belgian city its distinct and fascinating character. It's well known as the home of many international organizations, but what's not well known is that Brussels is a modest metropolis that reveals its splendid secrets slowly. It's a spontaneous city of neighborhoods that delights in the small pleasures of life. Walks along cobbled backstreets lead to generous green parks. Storied museums captivate visitors and sidewalk cafes come to life at the slightest ray of sunlight. If it's possible to present the magnificence of nineteenth-century architecture, and blend art nouveau and art deco masterpieces in a humble way, Brussels accomplishes it. It's a stimulating, multicultural crossroads that can—at times—be quiet and uncrowded. Here, the Axel Vervoordt Company shares two distinctive projects created for two separate families. One house is in a historic, architectural enclave. Informed by a philosophy of comfortable living in a metropolitan area with the unique charm of a village, Boris created the home based on feng shui influences. With a sense of youthful refined style, this home has a color palette developed from the earth's orientations. Modern art inspires, while cozy furniture creates inviting rooms. The second project is in a peaceful residential neighborhood. It's important to remember that iconic architects and designers including Victor Horta, Henry Van de Velde, Paul Hankar, and Jules Wabbes showed their talent for modern living in Brussels. Architect Marc Corbiau typifies the modernist tradition in a house built in the 1980s. The owners desired a contemporary space with the warmth of an old house. The team reinstated the family's art collection and the interior philosophy achieves a balance between living in the present with sleek, minimal lines, while being surrounded by objects from the past. An antique Italian library set is like a curiosity cabinet revealing its treasures. A mosaic-like tapestry made from recycled materials by the Ghanaian artist and sculptor El Anatsui expresses its beauty as it expands above the fireplace in the central drawing room; its title is *A Stitch in Time, II*, referring to the recuperation of old materials to create something new. Finding harmony in the balance of time is a central idea in this residence. Brussels is a contemporary canvas—where history meets modernity—upon which many varied stories are written. These homes contribute their narratives through art, personality, and grace.

PAGE 124

A mix of contemporary art and cozy furniture creates a refined and relaxed sitting room. The vases on the shelves in the foreground are glazed stoneware works from Parisian ceramist Sandra Zeenni (*Bouteilles blanches* [White Bottles], 2009, and *Bouteilles turquoise*, [Turquoise Bottles], 2010) and the ceramic objects are creations of French ceramist Nadia Pasquer (*Polyèdres*, 2010). Above the fireplace is a work by Dutch artist Kees Goudzwaard, who often creates trompe l'oeil paintings. The sculpture is a work by Belgian conceptual artist Michel François. The furniture includes Jean-Michel Frank and Axel Vervoordt club chairs.

LEFT

A large, lyrical painting from the *Waterfall* series from 1990 by American artist Pat Steir adds the element of water to the space. The furniture includes a stool by Le Corbusier, an early twentieth-century Scandinavian chair, and a few Axel Vervoordt Company creations including an Artempo cube, club chairs, and a sofa created in homage to Spanish fashion designer Mariano Fortuny y Madrazo. The sofa has fixed pillows in a complementary color scheme and sits next to the sunlit window.

FACING PAGE
Details of the home (from left to right): a 1950s stool in cerused oak; Devon & Devon
Fusion bathtub; the dialogue between a Le Corbusier stool, an Artempo cube, and the
Fortuny sofa by Axel Vervoordt; silvered architectural hardware by H. Theophile of New
York; a table by French architect and designer Jean Prouvé, with three sculptures on top:
an everyday nailing object by Sadaharu Horio, a puppet by Jeff Koons made for a charity
auction, and an untitled sphere by Michel François; a Scandinavian wooden chair designed
by a shipbuilder (Anonymous, c. 1920s); a painting by Keith Haring displayed in the owner's
dressing room; a detail of the dressing cabinet upholstered with aged leather panels;
a serene view of the central sitting room with a work by Kees Goudzwaard.

PAGES 130–31
Images of his and her bathroom creations. Light and reflection create a magical interplay
in a bathroom made of Indian white marble (p. 130). Guatemalan green marble, a bronze
mirror, and bronze taps by Dornbracht were selected to create a gentleman's bathroom (p. 131).

PAGES 132–33

Clean, modern lines, nature,
and light play an important role in
the second Brussels residence—a home
designed by architect Marc Corbiau.
An intriguing dialogue develops
between a sofa designed by
German-born American designer
Vladimir Kagan, a paintstick
drawing by American artist Richard
Serra, and a lamp by French designer
Serge Mouille (1922–88) (p. 132).
Light has a pure, ephemeral quality
as it streams through open doors
and a skylight window overhead;
in the background is the garden
designed by Belgian landscape
architect Erik Dhont and a sculpture
by British artist Tony Cragg (p. 133).

RIGHT

Art and architecture exist in
breathtaking harmony in a central
sitting room defined by an interior
philosophy that balances warmth with
intellectual curiosity, and classical
style with contemporary resonance.
Above the fireplace is a work by artist
El Anatsui titled *A Stitch in Time, II*.
Born in Ghana and active for most
of his career in Nigeria, he creates
sculptures made of humble materials
once destined for another purpose,
to create monumental tapestries that
make a personal statement about
a global world. Next to the fireplace
is a bronze vessel for the logs
created by Ibu Poilâne. The objects
and furniture include sofas by Belgian
designer Jules Wabbes (1919–74),
eighteenth-century French chairs,
an Axel Vervoordt coffee table,
and eighteenth-century candlesticks
from The Hague.

FACING PAGE
A source of wonder, art, and artifacts, a curiosity cabinet is a theater for
the memory and the mind. Here, a corner of the owner's cabinet reveals far-ranging
interests. A solid piece of amber is placed next to various pieces in a collection
of mushrooms. A seventeenth-century ivory nautilus-shell cup mingles with
a polyhedron and various other precious objects and memorabilia.

PAGE 138
In another corner of the cabinet, next to books, pictures, and other pieces,
a bronze sculpture surveys the room as if on the lookout. This portrait was created
during the time of Roman emperors Trajan and Hadrian, from 98–138 CE.

PAGE 139
This home blends contemporary architecture with classical style, and the late
eighteenth-century walnut bookcases house and display objects of various origins
like a veritable art exhibition. Bordering the central sitting room on either
side, the bookcases are of Italian Piemontese origin. This perspective also shows
the sofa by Jules Wabbes from another angle.

Come with me into the void.
Yves Klein (1928–62)

The endless expanse of sea and sky create a constantly changing canvas of color in the Côte d'Azur. The air is light and the light is magic. Each day has the power to transform by engaging the eye and liberating the senses. The climate and clarity of light along the Mediterranean has transformed artists and inspired residents for centuries, intensifying the pleasure of life along its shores. It was near Nice, along the Mediterranean of his youth, that artist Yves Klein developed a fascination for the void through witnessing the majesty of the sky and the power of the deep blue sea. Along a similar stretch of coastline, the new owner of a Belle Époque villa felt transported by the views—the sweeping fields of space—and reborn by the sun and proximity to the sea. Re-energized by long walks along cliffs carved from volcanic rocks and pathways bordered by white stones, he knew he had found a home for his family. Niçois architect Luc Svetchine rebuilt the villa and Boris Vervoordt conceived the interior to work in harmony with the scenery and the mystical effects of light. A sense of modernity exists in every detail of the home. Form is absolutely essential. Sofas, chairs, and tables designed by the Axel Vervoordt Company are paired with furniture made by some of the most iconic designers of the twentieth century. Objects were selected for their simplicity of form, clean lines, and precise detailing. The family's collection includes Greco-Roman sculptures and works of modern and contemporary art by Anish Kapoor, Lucio Fontana, Kazuo Shiraga, Hiroshi Sugimoto, Jef Verheyen, and, of course, Yves Klein—artists whose work seeks to understand our common humanity through exploring new dimensions in color, perspective, and matter. Next to the blue sea and under the big sky, this home nurtures creativity and the changing spirit of life.

PAGE 140

The terrace frames a view
of the sea and sky as they meet
to form a boundless horizon behind
a veiled female torso in white
marble with a sandy, pinkish patina
(Greek, early Hellenistic period, late
fourth century BCE). With a translucent
veil that covers the right side of
her face, the extraordinary life-sized
figure is remarkable for many reasons,
including the quality of the draped
folds that create a play of light
and shadow. The sculpture is most
likely a representation of Demeter,
goddess of the harvest.

PAGES 142–43

The elements of the sea, the sky,
and water from the swimming
pool merge in a magical view that
creates a sense of void and infinity.
Nice-based French architect
Luc Svetchine designed the pool.

RIGHT

An outdoor sitting room offers
views of the Mediterranean Sea.
The furniture includes Pierre Jeanneret
chairs designed for Panjab University
in Chandigarh, India, and a low
free-form table by French architect
and designer Charlotte Perriand
(1903–99), in the foreground.
Complementary furniture by
Sutherland and contemporary pieces
from the Axel Vervoordt Home
Collection, as well as an Artempo
cube, offer comfort and relaxation
to fully enjoy the scenery.

FACING PAGE
In front of the window overlooking the sea and garden is a white marble torso
of Venus (Roman, first century BCE–first century CE). This soft and sensuous statue
is related to ancient Greek sculptor Praxiteles's fully nude Aphrodite of Knidos
(c. 350 BCE). His female nudes were largely copied by the Romans in the first century
CE and were characterized by broad hips, flat stomachs, small breasts, and sloping
shoulders. Boris Vervoordt designed the round table, made specifically for this home
in white limestone, as an homage to English sculptor Henry Moore. On top of the table
is *Coupe à Glace* (Ice-Cream Dish, 2010) by Belgian artist Annick Tapernoux, created
in hammered silver and presenting flowers from the garden. Pierre Jeanneret designed
the teak armchairs for Panjab University in Chandigarh (c. 1950–60).

PAGE 148
A large eighteenth-century silver bowl from South America rests atop a Table Bleue
(Blue Table, 1963) by French artist Yves Klein (1928–62); the production of this table,
based on a model designed by Klein in 1961, continued after the artist's death.

PAGE 149
Light fills the central sitting room from windows on all sides. An important
work by Yves Klein titled *IKB 115*, signed and dated 1959, hangs on the right wall.
The work embodies Klein's romanticized belief in the immaterial world. In the center
of the space is a pair of Klein's Plexiglas tables from 1963—Table Bleue and Table
Rose—from the estate of Jef Verheyen. On top of the rose table is a hammered silver
vase by Annick Tapernoux. The pair of teak armchairs and the Kangourou lounge chair
were made by Pierre Jeanneret for Panjab University in Chandigarh (1950 and 1960,
respectively). Rising up from the table in the background is the leg of a monumental
statue (Greek, Hellenistic period, third century BCE). The bronze sculpture is
a testament to the natural idealism of the human figure, developed by the Greeks.
The warm patina of the metal brings out the subtle modulation of form and nuanced,
lifelike detailing. Next to the leg is a group of Egyptian cylindrical alabaster vases
from the early Dynastic period and a sub-cylindrical vase in banded alabaster from
South Turkmenistan (Margiana culture, second millennium BCE). The sofa, club chair,
and Artempo cube in eighteenth-century walnut are creations by Axel Vervoordt.

LEFT
A triptych of large, movable
windows in a guest bedroom presents
a panoramic view of the home's
surrounding landscape. Charlotte
Perriand made the desk table in
varnished pine (c. 1937–47), as well
as this prototype of the Siège Pivotant
(Swivel Chair), model C II (c. 1928);
made of metal with an original
leather cushion, this is Perriand's
first model for the Swivel Chair C.
On the table is an untitled 2006 work
by Michel François made in silver
leaf and clay; parts of the edges and
top corners have been clawed away,
leaving a beautiful tension between
its two opposing material extremes.
The intention of the artist is to make
time visual, by seeing it through
different kinds of movement. Serge
Mouille made the metal floor lamp
(Lampadaire Simple, c. 1953) and Pierre
Jeanneret made the easy armchair
of teak and cane for Panjab University
in Chandigarh (c. 1950–60). In creating
the furniture, he mainly used local
materials and employed many of the
city's residents, incorporating native
craftsmanship into his designs.

Details of the home (from left to right): a teak and cane armchair by Pierre Jeanneret
for Panjab University in Chandigarh (c. 1950–60); a marble sculpture titled *Ellipsoïde*
by Dominique Stroobant—a Belgian artist working in Italy, who is able to translate his
questions born from curiosity into dream-images and inventions, and to transform these
into matter; light and shadow in the texture of a terrace wall; the head of a crowned Venus
made in Pentelic marble with a sand-yellow patina (Greek, Hellenistic period, fourth–third
century BCE); a close-up detail of a Daum table lamp made of translucent glass (c. 1920)
from the collection of Yves Saint Laurent and Pierre Bergé; a 1914 Steinway rosewood piano
in front of "Aegean Sea 506 Pilion," a photograph taken in 1990 by Japanese artist Hiroshi
Sugimoto; a close-up of the Daum table lamp's mineral, frosted, and crystallized appearance;
shadow creates a moving sculpture on a Pierre Jeanneret armchair from 1950; a full
view of Daum's table lamp. Daum produced pieces in the art deco style with a richness
of proportion, an accuracy of design, and a sublimation of materials.

PAGE 154

In the home's entrance hallway, in the background, is a 2002 sculpture made
of limestone and pigment by Anish Kapoor. As Kapoor explains, "The idea is to make
an object which is not an object, to make a hole in the space, to make something which
actually does not exist. Even more, the extraordinary appearance, loved and feared,
of a piece of void, at once finite and infinite, reactivates the symbolic contact between
inside and outside, earth and heaven, male and female, active and passive, conceptual
and physical, thus renewing the process of knowing." Japanese painter and Gutai
master Kazuo Shiraga's painting *Syungei*, created in 1990, hangs in the sitting room
in dialogue with Lucio Fontana's spherical *Concetto Spaziale, Natura* from 1959–60.
Le Corbusier and Pierre Jeanneret made the top of the side table from a solid slice of tree
trunk, probably from a mango tree. These tables could be found at various locations
in Chandigarh: in the Assembly library, in Pierre Jeanneret's personal residence where
Le Corbusier resided during his many stays, or in former coworkers' or friends' homes,
as is the case for this example. Jean Prouvé created the Visiteur chair, a unique variation
of the Kangourou version, in 1948.

PAGE 155

Lucio Fontana's *Concetto Spaziale, Natura* is one of a series of works made
by cutting a gash across a sphere of terra-cotta clay. He believed that the incision was
a "vital sign" signaling "a desire to make the inert material live." Fontana was concerned
with transformation, and the shifting yet indestructible density of matter.

PAGE 156

The wall lamp was designed
by Le Corbusier in 1954 and produced
by Guilux for the Palais des Filateurs
in Ahmedabad, India, the headquarters
for one of the most prominent
associations for Indian cotton mill
owners. An adjustable deflector
in sheet metal is covered on the inside
with shining aluminum sheeting
to serve as a reflector.

PAGE 157

Jean Prouvé designed the Visiteur
chair in 1942. Several variants and
models were made over a period
of fifteen years; this chair has an
enameled tube frame with a polished
light oak body and wooden slats.

RIGHT

A view of the horizon from
the master bedroom is revealed.
Representing the home's connection
to the ever-changing light is
Jef Verheyen's *Night and Day*,
a diptych or screen in lacquered
cardboard from 1964–65.

LEFT
The beauty of nature is present at all
hours of the day in the lady's bathroom
designed by Luc Svetchine. In front of
the picture window is a desk with three
drawers by French designer Jean-Michel
Frank (c. 1930). The art deco chair in
front of the desk was made to order
by the Axel Vervoordt Company.
Nakajima Yasumi made the bronze
vase next to the bathtub (Japan, Showa
Period c. 1930) and Ibu Poilâne designed
the high-square bronze vase next to
the hand basins. On top of the desk
is a 1930s table lamp made of chromed
metal and opal glass by German-born
French lighting designer Jean Perzel.
Inspired by Romanesque stained
windows, Perzel wanted to use electricity
in the same way the Romanesque
glassmakers caught the sun in their
work, so he used the light beams to
mask the source of their light. In order
to disperse the light in an even manner,
he developed a particular sort of matte
glass that had been sandblasted.
This glass was subsequently coated
with enamel for decorative purposes.

The reflections of the moon on one thousand rivers
are from the same moon: the mind must be full of light.
Hung Tzu-Ch'eng (fl. 1572–1620)

Sprawling skies and boundless light are among the gifts that the historic southern region of Portugal bestows upon its residents and guests. Renowned for the brilliant quality of its climate, the Algarve experiences more minutes of sunshine than nearly any other area in Europe, thanks to its special geographic location. Close to North Africa and influenced by the Mediterranean, the expansive Atlantic Ocean bathes its shores. Explorers and skilled navigators set sail from here. The light is generous and luminous. Even when the temperature soars in the summer months, there is an Atlantic breeze that softens the intensity. Sheltered from some of the harsher inland weather and the colder climates to the north, the Algarve has an exquisite appeal that's easy to see. One feels it immediately, and there is magic to be experienced year round. Two Northern European families, passionate golfers, chose to create their second homes here in this oasis of warmth. On a long coastline defined by its private character and impressive views, architect Bernard de Clerck designed the Palladian-style homes and the Vervoordt team created the living spaces with a philosophy based on comfort, elegance, and artistic surroundings. The homes have very open spaces so that one feels the weather and the balance of living indoors with the presence of the outdoor climate. In one home, classic beauty can be found in a collection of first- and second-century Roman antiquities. A sublime seventeenth-century Italian cupboard in sky blue is perfectly matched to this environment in which the skies are a strong, azure-blue all year round. The owners of the other residence have chosen some major works of the mid-twentieth century Japanese Gutai period, including masterpieces like a 1961 Kazuo Shiraga painting and Shozo Shimamoto's *Canon Picture* from 1957, along with a jewel-like white work by German artist Günther Uecker. In the study, eighteenth-century paneling was used to make a library in a room that blends an intellectual formality with a sense of relaxation and warmth. The shelves present an interesting collection of Margianan, Egyptian, and Roman artifacts as well as contemporary pieces. In both residences, light fills terraces and falls through windows as the pleasures of life unfold. There is an art to living, and here, in these homes, it's been found.

PAGE 162

In the main sitting room, works of art
from different periods and different
parts of the world come together.
At left, a small untitled work from
1960 by Günther Uecker was originally
a gift from the artist to his friend,
the Belgian painter Jef Verheyen.
Resting atop an eighteenth-century
oak chest of drawers is an Italian marble
bowl from the 1800s. Presiding in the
center is *Canon Picture* (1957) by Gutai
master and cofounder Shozo Shimamoto
(1928–2013). On the opposite side of
the doorway is a fragment of bronze
drapery (Greek, fourth–third century,
BCE), originally part of the lower half
of a life-sized sculpture of a charioteer.
The play of light and shadow, and
the deep folds of the draped textile
enhance its verticality.

RIGHT

This is the same sitting room seen
from a different angle. Here, a 1960
painting in oil on canvas from another
of the founding members of the
Gutai movement is shown—*Tentaisei
Sonshiko* (Powerful Tiger) by Kazuo
Shiraga. On the sculptor's stand next
to the window is a large stoneware vase
with a natural ash glaze by Japanese
artist and potter Shiro Tsujimura.
The furniture in the room includes
a selection from the Axel Vervoordt
Home Collection, including a club chair,
canapé, folding stools, and a low
walnut coffee table. The refined walnut
wingchair is French *Régence* (early
eighteenth-century). The additional
objects include a petrified wood stand,
a granite bowl from the Margiana
culture (second millennium BCE),
a nest of six fossilized dinosaur eggs
embedded in its original clay sediment
(China, 100–65 million years ago),
a Chinese Han Dynasty terra-cotta
vase lamp (206 BCE–220 CE), and an
eighteenth-century French wooden chest.

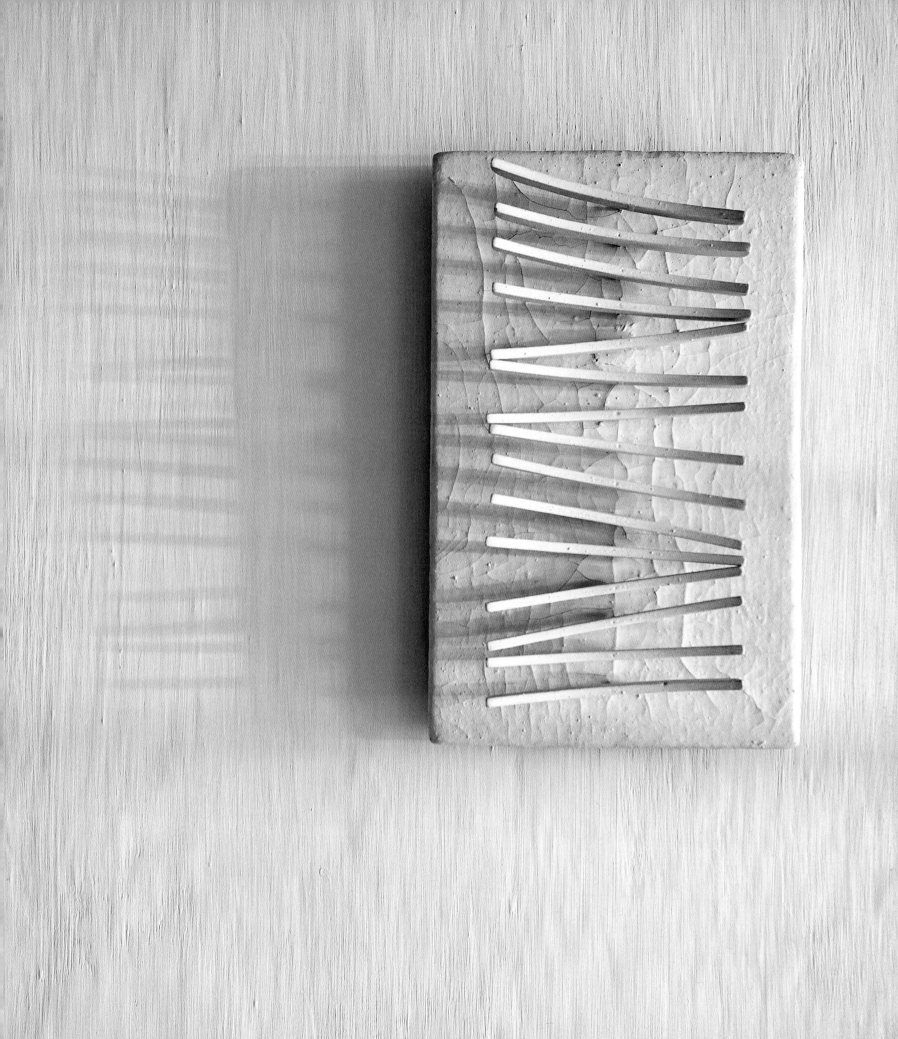

PAGE 166
A detail of Kazuo Shiraga's action painting *Tentaisei Sonshiko* (Powerful Tiger). One of the leading figures of Japan's avant-garde Gutai movement, Shiraga painted with his feet—a technique that provided a physical connection with his material and was a direct expression of his art, which redefined space, performance, and painting.

PAGE 167
A close-up of Günther Uecker's untitled 1960 work using painted wood and tempera on canvas.

LEFT

The family's neoclassical Italian library is a warm, enlightening space that houses books and many Egyptian, Roman, and Middle Eastern archaeological objects. An overview of particularly interesting pieces (from the left) includes a collection of alabaster bowls and goblets; column idols in white and black marble (Margiana culture, second millennium BCE); an ancient Syrian bowl of diorite rock with a sand crust patina (third millennium BCE); and a fragment of a draped woman's torso in marble (Roman, second–third century CE). In the center is a small, pear-shaped Egyptian serpentine vase (c. 1550–1070 BCE), as well as a fragmentary face of the pharaoh Amenemhat III made in indurated limestone (Egypt, c. 1853–1806 BCE). At right is a fragment of a block statue made in limestone with traces of polychromy and the head of a block statue made in light gray granodiorite (Egypt, Late Period, XXVI Dynasty, 664–525 BCE), as well as a collection of marble Kusura idols, which are part of a long Anatolian tradition of fertility figures (Turkey, c. 3000–2000 BCE). The furnishings include early nineteenth-century English end tables, a two-thousand-year-old Chinese Han ceramic jar transformed into a lamp, and Axel Vervoordt Company sofas.

PAGES 170–71
Light, shadow, and peaceful garden views overlooking the water can be seen from
the loggia, or outdoor terrace. In a home that blends art with the elements of nature,
this space represents the harmony of the house's interior and exterior.

FACING PAGE
The sun shines on an exterior dining space and spills into the kitchen, which includes
eighteenth-century German cabinets that once belonged to the counts of Baden-Baden.

PAGES 174–75
This double-page spread showcases two opposing views of the same room in the
second residence built by architect Bernard de Clerck. The space combines high, arched
ceilings and a tropical, water-resistant terrace floor. When the windows and doors are
open, one feels the comfort of a room exposed to the elements of nature. On cooler days,
a fireplace adds warmth and ambience. Among the furnishings are pieces from the
Axel Vervoordt Home Collection and a Chinese terra-cotta vase (c. 480–220 BCE) (p. 174).
The furniture includes an early eighteenth-century Baroque walnut console table and
a seventeenth-century French chest in leather along with Axel Vervoordt Company
creations (p. 175). On top of the coffee table, there is a large wooden bowl and a pair
of Indian slate vessels. Placed on the chest is an ornamental funerary turban in white
marble from the Ottoman Empire (seventeenth century). On the right, an ink-on-paper
work titled *Atarimae-no-koto* (A Matter of Course) by Sadaharu Horio hangs above
the fireplace. Horio is a Japanese artist who each day—from the moment he awakes
to the time he goes to sleep—creates works that he calls *Ordinary Things*.

Live in the sunshine, swim the sea, drink the wild air's salubrity.
Ralph Waldo Emerson (1803–82)

If light is the energy of the world, water is its transformation, and together they create magic. At night, moonlight dances on the waves and surface of the sea, streaming through like fingers caressing its unreachable depths. During the day, the oceans reflect the sky in an infinite dialogue that blends the ingredients of sunlight, air, water, and clouds with the shore's landscape and the hues of the horizon. The sea stirs creativity and seems to cure what ails. Even when it may be calm, it's never still. As John F. Kennedy said, "We are tied to the ocean. And when we go back to the sea, whether it is to sail or to watch it, we are going back from whence we came." This concept of returning to one's origins is central to the interior philosophy for a yacht that strives for balance between the pleasures of escape and the perspectives of life. Even when there's a party, being at sea naturally inspires introspection. The boat needed to be a relaxing space for family, friends, and invited guests, and the owners also wanted it to be a place for study, contemplation, and sharing knowledge—a moving space intended for creative, conversational salons and the birthplace of new ideas. The Axel Vervoordt Company refitted an original design by Carlo Nuvolari and Dan Lenard. Objects that refer to the origins of humanity were chosen from the family's collection and found a new home on board. A five-thousand-year-old Yemenite female fertility idol at the entrance to the vessel is an open and welcoming gesture. A painting by Belgian artist Jef Verheyen inspired by Egypt is paired with a pre-dynastic Egyptian alabaster vase. Chairs, a table, and library shelves by Belgian designer Jules Wabbes are combined with armchairs by French designer Eugene Printz. Natural materials help create sensual experiences. Comfort is paramount. Interior cabins and rooms blend with distinctive exterior spaces in a seamless style that reflects both male and female sensibilities. There is a playful elegance throughout. On this boat, mornings are spent lingering at the breakfast table, afternoons take shape while cruising the seas with the music turned up, and evenings evolve outside while witnessing the sun's daily disappearance as it transforms the horizon. This is a boat that roams the earth's oceans while guests experience the pleasures of freedom, the relaxation of escape, and the pure exhilaration of the open air. The salt of the sea cures the body and traveling regenerates the soul. Even when it remains in view, the shore often feels far away.

PAGE 176

The sun sets behind a mountainous landscape, and the changing sky reflects light on the constantly moving surface of the sea. A group of boats sets anchor for the evening, evocative of floating jewels.

PAGE 178

A comfortable, double-sided U-shaped sofa, designed by the Axel Vervoordt Company for the vessel in collaboration with Sinot Yacht Design, offers space for conversation and relaxation during a cruise.

PAGE 179

In the background is another perspective of the sofa on the outer bridge deck. In the sitting room is a Rippen Grand Piano from the Netherlands and a selection of Axel Vervoordt Company furniture. Just behind the sofa is the 1993 *Rice House* by German artist Wolfgang Laib.

LEFT

In the background, overlooking the main sitting room, is Jef Verheyen's 1978 *Grote Concorde* (Large Concord) in dialogue with an Egyptian alabaster bottle placed atop a Jules Wabbes dresser (c. 1965). The furniture includes a dining table with a solid round top in crosscut wood with five bronze legs and a series of six leather and metal chairs, also by Jules Wabbes (c. 1970). To the right is a pair of 1935 armchairs by French art deco designer Eugène Printz (1889–1948). In the center is an eighteenth-century English open armchair. In the foreground and on the left, a wide chair and sofa by French designer Christian Liaigre flank an Axel Vervoordt walnut coffee table.

PAGE 182

In the master bedroom, a chair from the Axel Vervoordt Collection sits beside
Superficie Bianca (White Surface) by Enrico Castellani, signed, titled, and dated 1970.

PAGE 183

A detail of Castellani's relief painting. Part of an Italian movement that began
in the 1960s with the purpose of developing a new type of visual language, Castellani
became known for his two-dimensional works formed by fastening canvas over protruding
nails to allow for changes in positive and negative space, in light, and in shade.

FACING PAGE

Details of the boat (from left to right): a rounded corner of the wooden frame
of the double-sided U-shaped sofa on the outer bridge deck; a Venus statue in white
marble (Roman, first–second century CE), related to Praxiteles's fully nude *Aphrodite
of Knidos* (c. 350 BCE); an elegant, well-hollowed black porphyry jar (Egyptian, early
Dynastic period, c. 3100–2686 BCE); the reflection of light and a view of the sea from
a guest cabin during a cruise; a pair of 2006 glass vases by Venetian artist Massimo
Micheluzzi, an Italian artist who blends ancient Murano techniques with a contemporary
vision; a detailed view of *Twisted Strings—Phase I – II – III*, a work made with painted cotton
on a frame by Walter Leblanc, one of Belgium's most representative kinetic artists; a small
Egyptian tub pot in banded alabaster (Late Period, XXVIth–XXXIst Dynasty, 664–332 BCE)
with delicate veining, precise workmanship, and a beautiful finish; an Egyptian block statue
of "Pa-di-Imen-neb-nesut-tawy" made with indurated limestone on a thick rectangular
base, with the figure's knees up and arms folded to indicate patience (Ptolemaic Dynasty,
305–30 BCE); a 2009 earthenware and porcelain work by French artist Nadia Pasquer.

PAGE 186

The magical dialogue between light and water as seen from the main deck.

PAGE 187

A standing female figure sculpted from a large, single piece of granite
(South Arabian, third–second millennium BCE). Bronze Age idols such as this
are often found in the Yemeni highlands and represent the oldest evidence
of anthropomorphic sculpture in ancient Yemen.

PAGES 188–89

The sun rises over the bay of Cannes as a new day begins. The furniture on the main
deck was designed in collaboration with the Axel Vervoordt Company, Amells, and Glyn
Peter Machin. On the table is an enameled porcelain vase designed by French ceramist
Jean Girel titled *Hommage à Patinir* (Tribute to Patinir). Joachim Patinir was a Flemish
painter who specialized in landscape paintings.

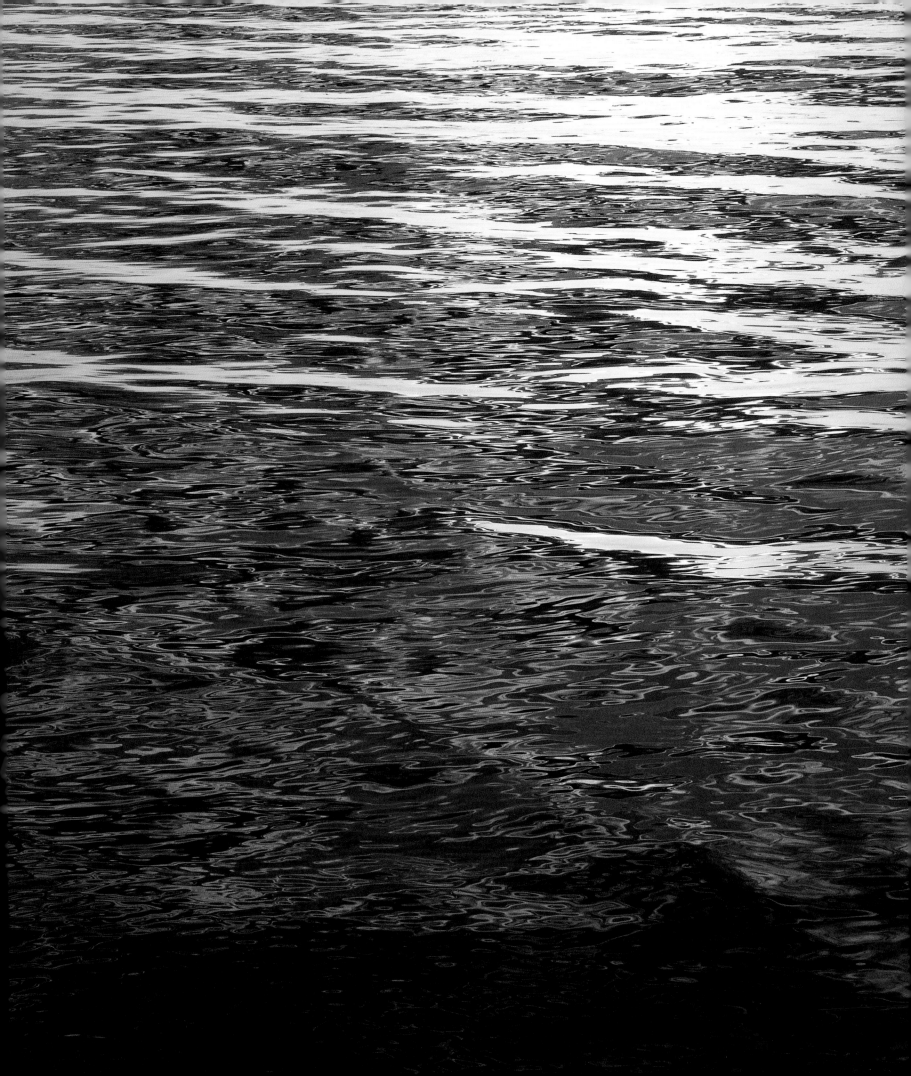

We shall not cease from exploration
And the end of all our exploring
Will be to arrive where we started
And know the place for the first time.
T.S. Eliot (1888–1965), "Little Gidding," *Four Quartets*, 1943

Munich is the capital city of Bavaria and is located on the Isar River, north of the Alps. The crisp, rushing water from the mountains feeds the river and the river feeds the character of the city, providing picturesque backdrops for the pleasures of life. With medieval origins, Munich balances tradition with modernity. This is a forward-thinking place that's renowned for its quality of life. Parks, pedestrian avenues, market squares, and cafés invite residents into the light as soon as the weather permits and give this city its distinctive character. The gently winding banks of the Isar split the city into sections, creating unique islands while offering playful spots for recreation. For those not lucky enough to live there, how is it best to experience its warmth and charm? In the center of this city is a grand hotel named the Bayerischer Hof. Hotels, by their nature, are islands within a city and must bridge a gap that often seems insurmountable—they must be luxurious enough to lure you away from home but as soon as you walk in the front doors, they must be approachable, elegant places that *feel* like home. With timeless spirit and cultivated service, the Bayerischer Hof accomplishes this. Founded in 1841 and owned by the Volkhardt family for more than a hundred years, Innegrit Volkhardt asked the Axel Vervoordt team to be part of a renovation project. The goal was to reimagine an existing restaurant, dividing it into two new culinary spaces. Axel named the first restaurant Atelier, an intimate space built with the philosophy of a workshop. Art proved to be essential in these spaces for a sense of character and spirituality. Belgian artist and scientist Dirk Vander Eecken known for creating an "Art of the Unseen" was commissioned to create abstract paintings on mobile walls. There are terrazzo floors, and walls painted with natural earth tones. In these spaces, every detail from the reception room to the service materials was determined and created. Furniture was crafted from antique materials. In the Garden restaurant, a workshop theme continues, with exposed technical features and a greenhouse built with an industrial iron finish. Materials were recuperated and have been transformed in the service of their new setting. In these spaces, culinary excellence reigns, while comfort and artistry nourish the other senses. Light exists in the shade of a garden terrace and through the shadows of private dining rooms that have a secret and special emotion. There is a heightened sense of creativity throughout. In a hotel rooted in history and prized for its warmth paired with a discreet sense of luxury, these projects tell new stories while continuing grand traditions.

PAGE 190

On warmer days, a large garden terrace welcomes guests to dine outdoors
in the sunlight. The workshop atmosphere created indoors extends outside, as seen
in the industrial choices made here with strong iron tables and armchairs.

PAGES 192–93

This double-page spread showcases the warm interior dining spaces. On the wall
hangs a woman's wool mantle or Nañaka (1850–1920) (p. 192). The Nañaka is only found
in and around the village of Toropalca in the state of Chuquisaca in Bolivia. They are
historically made from natural black or dark brown sheep's wool and over-dyed with
cochineal or charcoal, and they are used for ceremonial occasions. A long view shows
the composition of the dining room and the exhibited works of art (p. 193). Belgian
artist Dirk Vander Eecken designed the mobile doors, titled *The Door of Invisibility*,
specially for the hotel. Inspired by an enlarged image of the carbon atom, he created
a functional work that explores the tension between order and chaos. On the back
wall are two Korean textile fragments and an indigo blue Japanese textile. The chairs
and serving tables are Axel Vervoordt Company creations.

FACING PAGE

Details of the restaurant (from left to right): the aged texture of wood resembles
an abstract painting; a handcrafted detail of a Lady Gainsborough desk chair, part
of the Axel Vervoordt Home Collection; a detail of a serving table made by the Vervoordt
workshop and used in the garden restaurant; a 2008 lacquer-on-canvas painting by Dirk
Vander Eecken—the grids and patterns he uses result in abstract, almost indefinable
paintings that possess many layers referring to the visible and invisible, from finite
to infinite; a late eighteenth-century French artist's mannequin with a beautiful patina;
a wooden sculptor's stand from c. 1900; a rhomboidal dodecahedron sits atop a French
artist's stand in oak; wine glasses glisten in the light; a hanging lamp created by the Axel
Vervoordt Company completes the workshop atmosphere.

PAGE 196

A close-up detail of aged wood and flaked paint is evocative of an abstract Artempo painting.

PAGE 197

A relaxing seating area for restaurant guests demonstrates the harmony of the interior
philosophy, which strives for a balance between a creative workshop atmosphere and
industrial influences. On the left, a sixteenth-century French or German iron anvil is placed
on top of a French wood and iron artist's stand. Axel Vervoordt creations include a sofa,
a coffee table made from seventeenth-century Italian chestnut planks, and ancient wood
Artempo cubes. On the wall is a pair of French frameworks, which are delicately constructed
scale models of roof constructions. These *pièces de maîtrise* (literally "masterpieces"),
as they are called, were made by apprentices of certain *métiers*, or trades, to demonstrate
their technical ingenuity, in order to be accepted as masters in their profession.

Art is the elimination of the unnecessary.
Pablo Picasso (1881–1973)

In a home filled with light, the shadows on white walls and bare floors become like paintings—communicating the complex patterns of nature in an ever-evolving dialogue with the changing sunlight. Surrounded by lush green forests on a rising hilltop in the south of France, the air carries the fragrant scents of the area's signature flowers. It was in this house, in a small ancient village, that Pablo Picasso lived and worked. The son of Spain, the incomparably talented and towering figure who revolutionized art in the twentieth century, Picasso spent the latter part of his life in a home and studio here, not far from Cannes. The space was created as he imagined, in collaboration with the French architect Jacques Couëlle, with large windows allowing clear and consistent light to penetrate the house at all hours of the day. As Picasso once said, "Every act of creation is first of all an act of destruction." For a European family, the question that arose was how to create a home in the very same rooms in which Picasso had once lived, while retaining a sense of the artist's energy and the very present soul of the spaces. After a great deal of reflection, Axel concluded that the key to making such a strong, important house livable was through simplicity. Keep it simple—preserve the artist's atmosphere, for artists are the ones who see what others don't. These spaces have clarity, purity, and an impeccable stillness. One can almost hear the silence and witness light as it bends, stretches, expands, and explores. This is a home that's not empty, but filled only with what is essential, with objects that the house deigns to accept: a seventeenth-century Italian notary's desk weathered over time through devoted use; a reflective work by Anish Kapoor; a trio of hollow stones, formerly used by a shepherd as receptacles for his animals' feed. The generous, light-filled spaces echo a minimalism that's informed by a restraint of purpose. The architecture is not solely concerned with form for the sake of beauty, it's also focused on allowing abundant light to permeate the house and illuminate the soul of the space. Axel's vision of the void offers perspective on these spaces and what he calls the fullness of the emptiness. These are calm, quiet, creative rooms. Windows are like framed paintings that offer a master's vision of a green landscape and a village whose name says it all: *Notre-Dame-de-Vie—Our Lady of Life*. The home is a light, white space, resembling a bare canvas. In these rooms, one feels a certain kind of force of gravity, connecting us through the present to the past—and, always, to the artist.

PAGE 198

In order to preserve a sense of the soul of Picasso's former (and final) home, the rooms contain only essential elements, and works that the spaces could accept. Here, light, architecture, and a stainless steel work by Anish Kapoor from 2006 offer plenty to contemplate. Kapoor's mirror-like work distorts the viewer and the surroundings, offering an intriguing sense of engagement while evoking awe and fascination through the work's reflective facade.

LEFT

In collaboration with architect Jacques Couëlle, the rooms were created as Picasso imagined, with clear and consistent light. One senses the artist's connection with light and landscape through the large sliding windows that bring nature into the owner's bedroom. The furniture includes an eighteenth-century Italian pine chest, a pine cupboard from Tuscany, a seventeenth- to eighteenth-century Italian stool, a 1950s Scandinavian rosewood chair, and a nineteenth-century French wine table. The serene earthenware vases are Korean (eighteenth–nineteenth century) and Japanese (Edo Period, 1603–1867, and Meiji Period, 1868–1912).

PAGES 202–3
The staircase winds upward through the home's layers, ascending toward the light.
Below the original arched ceiling is a French wooden table and a nineteenth-century French
bowl (p. 202). One senses Axel's philosophy of creating fullness from emptiness with
these sparse, reflective rooms (p. 203). Here, a nineteenth-century Chinese root vase made
in burr wood sits atop a chestnut folding table from Burgundy (c. 1700).

FACING PAGE
A trio of hollow stone and granite basins are like sculptures installed next to
a window, as light pours into the room. Originally used by a shepherd in the Italian Alpine
region, these basins helped keep the animals' food fresh and protected.

PAGE 206
There is a strong luminous presence in this room, as sunlight floods through
the circular windows and doors. The artist's soul is recalled through the presence
of a seventeenth-century Italian notary's desk, worn over time through devoted use.
The desk was included in the exhibition Artempo: Where Time Becomes Art, curated by Axel
Vervoordt at the Palazzo Fortuny in Venice, which explored the relationship between time
and art. On top of the desk is a marble ovoid idol (Margiana culture, second millennium
BCE). The middle Bronze Age culture of ancient Margiana flourished in western Central
Asia, which was rich in raw materials. Also on the desk is a pair of black jade stones from
the Chinese mountains; black jade is often thought to be a protective stone that helps
a person look inward while absorbing and transforming energy.

PAGE 207
This detail of the desk is evocative of an abstract painting—the ravages of time thus create art.

Architecture is the reaching out for truth.
Louis Kahn (1901–74)

Full of innumerable mysteries and reaching unfathomable depths, the sea transfixes us with its poetry and transports us with its power. Covering a vast majority of the earth's surface, the ocean is at once the great border that divides nations and the boundless bridge that connects them. A vehicle for trade, travel, and leisure, the seas rewarded skilled explorers with stories, bounty, and beauty. In Greek mythology, Poseidon represents the power and unpredictable patterns of the sea with his untamed creative spirit. He was a mature god who ruled the sea and lived in an underwater palace. The creatures of the deep were created by his imaginative hand and travelers were controlled at the whim of his trident as he sailed the waves on a horse-drawn chariot. When calm, the oceans offered fishermen and explorers an exhilarating experience. Seduced by the freedom of holidays at sea, a family undertook what they knew would be a lifetime project and a dream come true: to create a home on the water. They wanted a place where their family, friends, and guests could share their passion for seeing the world while sailing. The key to the design was to create a sense of freedom in every element, expressing a distinctive character with a depth of feeling, true personality, and a sense of purity. The concepts and overall philosophy here are driven by an intriguing duality of art deco and industrial design infused with a modern view of man's individual strength and creative will. Objects have a straight-lined beauty and purity of form. Sparseness gives space for the light. Large windows are like stages for the horizon and sea views. Every boat is a feat of engineering and a complex mix of metal and moving parts, while remaining a machine of classical grace. Metal studs, beams, and technical components were purposefully left bare. Like a house showing its pillars, the machine exposes its structure in victory, proud of its modern beauty. The interior philosophy strives for balance. These are comfortable, livable spaces that are free of ostentation. Luxury exists in the refined elegance and sensuality of materials—hand-woven silks, premium leathers, and the artful textures of walnut. Seeking harmony with water and light, this is a very personal home of simple, profound elegance that is constantly moving, a passionate exploration in search of the majesty, wonder, and magnificence of the earth.

PAGE 208

Panoramic windows offer boundless views of the sea and sky. Paired with a hand-woven silk carpet, the large mahogany sofa from France (1930–40) and the Ski Bar coffee table (c. 1930) were both made by French architect, designer, and decorator Paul Dupré-Lafon (1900–71). He was primarily known for his fusion of luxurious materials, such as exotic woods and leathers, with a minimalist architectural sensibility. A fine example, the bar rests on runner-shaped feet in gilt metal, the top is black opaline, and storage spaces are covered in red leather. Next to an early nineteenth-century German armchair is a bronze floor lamp by Vilhelm Lauritzen (1894–1984), a Danish modernist architect who believed architecture must not limit itself to architectural function or aesthetics.

PAGE 210

On the dining room bookshelves is a trio of Egyptian early Dynastic alabaster vessels, including an offering table stand and two bowls (Old Kingdom, IVth Dynasty, c. 2450–2300 BCE). One of the glories of ancient Egyptian craftsmanship was the making of stone vessels. Even the hardest stones were carved with extraordinary precision and assurance. The material allowed the sculptor to indulge the Egyptian penchant for understatement, allowing the shape of objects and the materials from which they were made to speak for themselves.

PAGE 211

Above the dining room table hangs *Haar der Nymphen* (Nymphs' Hair, 1964) by Günther Uecker. To create works such as this, Uecker would kneel on the untouched surface and start hammering the nails spontaneously, without a preliminary sketch, working outward from the center at a rapid, rhythmic pace. The energetic dynamism of the creative process remains palpable in the finished work. The Axel Vervoordt Company designed the table in tropical wood with bronze, column-shaped legs and four separate tops for a versatile length. Pierre Jeanneret designed the armchairs in mahogany and cane. In the early 1950s, Le Corbusier and his cousin Jeanneret started their urban planning project in Chandigarh, India, producing low-cost buildings for the new town. Jeanneret stayed for fifteen years and the city evolved into a landmark of modern architecture.

FACING PAGE

Details of the home (from left to right): for the sports bar, Dominique Stroobant created a white, fiberglass sculpture; a Boule table lamp in nickel-plated metal (1930) by French designer Félix Aublet (1903–78); a textured, detailed view of eighteenth-century sheets of walnut from an Italian monastery, used to create wall-mounted cabinetry; the belly of a sandstone sculpture, probably of a life-sized torso of Maitreya—a popular deity and messianic Bodhisattva widely worshipped as the Buddha of the future (Thailand, Koh Ker style, tenth century CE); an office armchair by Pierre Jeanneret; the rounded corner detail of the Paul Dupré-Lafon sofa; a mahogany lounge chair with ivory-colored cotton webbing created by Japanese-American designer George Nakashima in the 1960s; light and shadow outdoors; a pair of Jeanneret natural oak and cane *chauffeuses basses*—low chairs to be placed by the fireplace—originally part of a four-piece set ordered by the architect Michel Weill for his home.

PAGE 214

Hot morning coffee served
in a cup by French tableware designer
Murielle Grateau, on a tray created
by the Axel Vervoordt Company.

PAGE 215

A lounge daybed offers a comfortable
place for relaxing, watching television,
or reading under a Serge Mouille
lamp. An untitled photogram by English
photographer Adam Fuss from 1989
hangs above a pair of earthenware
works (c. 1960) by Italian ceramist
Carlo Zauli (1926–2002). The furniture
in the room includes a chest of drawers
made of rosewood and brass, an
armchair, and a unique round desk
table with a right-cut edge, all dating
from 1950 to the late 1960s and
designed by Jules Wabbes.

LEFT

A guest cabin features walls
covered with vegetal tinted leather
and three windows overlooking the
sky and sea. On the left is a wood and
leather Bambi armchair designed by
Rastad and Relling (Norway, c. 1960)
and a Chinese plum vase (Yuan
Dynasty, c. 1300). This type of celadon
pottery was first made in China,
where potters discovered that when
ash landed on ceramic works being
fired in kilns at a high temperature,
the result was a wonderful green
finish. The desk furniture includes
an art deco chair from the Axel
Vervoordt Home Collection and a 1930
Boule table lamp by Félix Aublet.
Above the desk is a 1962 work titled
Long Island by Le Corbusier.
To create the drawing, he painted
a transparent sheet of cellulose acetate
black and etched his drawing into
it using a knife, like a sort of negative.

Once we believe in ourselves,
we can risk curiosity, wonder, spontaneous delight,
or any experience that reveals the human spirit.
E.E. Cummings (1894–1962)

If the currency of creativity is curiosity, Manhattan has an endless supply of both. It's the oldest and smallest of New York's five boroughs, but the only one that's known simply as "the city." It's an island borough, bound by water on all sides, a majestic place unto itself that would be mythological if it weren't so magnificently real. Rising in a mass of concrete, glass, steel, and pure ambition, Manhattan is inspiring and intimidating, chaotic and dense, restless and captivating, modern and magnetic. Many stories are told here of chance encounters, seized opportunities, and one-of-a-kind experiences. It's a creative universe unto itself, and one in which the laws of life are surprising and can't always be readily explained. That's the beauty of its diverse, human character. Paris may be the City of Light, but New York is the city that never turns the lights out. Discovery beckons around every corner. The city moves at the speed of light and its pace requires perspective. This is what a home provides—a place that balances the sounds in the streets with silence, privacy, and distinctive personal taste. In a Manhattan apartment, the Vervoordt team provided a fashion designer and collector with antiquities, furniture, and carefully placed artworks within an enriching color palette. Defined by a truly unique taste, the owner collects sixteenth- and seventeenth-century Old Master drawings, modern and contemporary drawings, photographs, and sculpture, all of exceptional quality. Decisions were made to complement their presence in every room. It was a collaborative process with a curator's touch. The collection has been built throughout the course of the owner's fascinating life. He has the eye of a creative and curious individual who knows exactly what he wants to express, and, in the process, rediscovers himself every time. Experiencing this home and its collection of art with this in mind is reminiscent of a camera obscura—a black box into which light enters through a pinhole, revealing the outside world and rendering images visible. With the invention of photography, artists defined their medium and then advanced it. Each work of art is a whole world unto itself. Drawings on paper reflect the artist's close interaction with the medium. There's a balance of technique, artistry, and context evident in every room. This is the creative home of a collector that responds to the immediacy of draftsmanship—in a dazzling city that understands it all.

PAGE 218

The warm sitting room showcases
an impressive collection of works on
paper, starting with Californian artist
Ed Ruscha's 1968 *Clock* (top left).
Below it is a collage by German painter
and sculptor Anselm Kiefer.
To the left of the window is a 1913
collage by Pablo Picasso titled
*Verre et Bouteille de Bass sur une
Table* (Glass and Bass Bottle on
a Table), and on the right is an untitled
1960 drawing by British artist Ben
Nicholson (1894–1982). Above the
fireplace is a 1982 paintstick-on-paper
work by Richard Serra titled *Canadian
Pacific*. The furniture includes sofas
and coffee tables from the Axel
Vervoordt Home Collection and two
English Regency armchairs inspired
by Thomas Hope drawings.

RIGHT

Standing guard in the entrance
hallway, a bronze bust with a brown
patina by Alberto Giacometti,
titled *Diego au Manteau* (Diego
in a Coat)—conceived in 1954 and cast
in 1959—welcomes guests to the home.
On the left is a photogram by Adam
Fuss from the 1992 series "Details
of Love." On the right is *L'Aberrateur*
(The Deviant), a 1963 drawing by
French artist Jean Dubuffet (1901–85).
On the floor is an untitled 1943
watercolor by German-born American
artist Hans Hofmann (1880–1966).
In the background, light from two
windows frames a large-scale Yemenite
figure in alabaster (Sabaean Kingdom,
first century BCE–first century CE),
a type of funerary figure.

A paper collage and black ink work by Jean Dubuffet titled *Barbe de Voyance* (Clairvoyant Beard), from 1959.

PAGE 223
In a gray and white dining room is a black lacquer table by Jules Wabbes.
On the left is *Leonardo Pisano* (2007) by Anselm Kiefer, and on the right is print "#14" (2000) from the "New Abstraction" series by American artist James Welling.

FACING PAGE
Details of the home (clockwise from top left): a monumental head of the Empress Livia (Roman, late first century BCE–early first century CE). The wife of Emperor Augustus and the mother of Emperor Tiberius, Empress Livia played a major role in Roman politics—this sculpture, with its original patina, is a portrait of her as a young woman; a view of the hallway corridor displays the owner's photography collection; a bronze sculpture by Joan Miró from 1968 titled *Tête* (Head); a detailed view of the drawing cabinet reveals *Head of a Woman Wearing a Ghirlanda* by Florentine artist Baccio Bandinelli (1493–1560).

RIGHT

A roaring fire warms the drawing
room, a space for sharing conversation
while surrounded by works of art.
Above the fireplace is a 1985 graphite
pencil-on-paper work by Ed Ruscha
titled *Words Going Round #3*. Mannerist
drawings on the window wall include
The Blood of Christ Redeems the World
(1628–31) by Genovese artist Giulio Benso
(top right), and on the right wall is a small
watercolor-and gouache-on-vellum portrait
of a small dog titled *An Affenpinscher*
(1580), by sixteenth-century German
artist Hans Hoffmann. On the far right
is a painting by Helen Frankenthaler
(1928–2011), an American painter known
for her lyrically abstract works.

PAGE 228

A view of Manhattan is reflected
against a cut, collaged, and mounted
gelatin silver print "Barbershop
Cutout #2, West Palm Beach, Fl." (1940)
by American photographer Arnold
Newman (1918–2006).

PAGE 229

Light and shadow from the window
enter the master bedroom. A large,
untitled photogram by English artist
Adam Fuss shows a reflection from
the building outside. Against the door
is a photograph by Hiroshi Sugimoto
titled "Kunsthaus Bregenz—Peter
Zumthor" (2000–2001). A Japanese
artist living and working in Tokyo and
New York, Sugimoto explores through
his photographs the relationship
between photography, light, and time,
as well as examining the ineffable
nature of reality. The reflection of the
1970s chrome furniture adds to the
element of light and lightness in this
space. In the corridor in the background,
a collection of early twentieth-century
photographs related to drawing and
graffiti is displayed.

The sun shines not on us but in us.
John Muir (1838–1914)

Fluid in its beauty and awesome in its force, the water of the oceans captures and reflects the light of the sun in an endlessly changing composition. It's an art to witness as one stands close to the sea, on the shores. On a stunning stretch of coastline in New England, the power, beauty, and majesty of nature make a deep and profound impression. It was here that an American family wanted a residence in which nature would always be present. This region is a place that brims with stories of America's origins. It's an important part of the country's history, but also seems to exist outside of it in a timeless dialogue with nature, the sea, and the changing seasons. The project developed on the site of a nineteenth-century mansion, and the house was built next to the water. As you pass through each room, the scenery develops in front of you. The views give the impression that you are floating on the water. Light is thick, dense, and transcendent. The spaces are free and open. This is a home where the empty spaces are the true art. The void is energy and an unseen power that exists between objects. Together with Cutler Anderson Architects, the Axel Vervoordt team's role was to choose materials that created a sense of peace and timelessness. Every detail was carefully considered and every choice thoughtfully made. Materials were prized not soley for their elegance, but also for their natural properties, with the intention that they should age well and allow the home to grow increasingly beautiful. The objects selected could be ancient or modern, but they all needed to possess a certain simplicity and a noble proportion, and be free from ostentation. As the preferred indigenous wood, oak was chosen for cabinetry designs. Antique stones from Italy, used for flooring and terraces, look as if they've always been part of the property. The library was made from reclaimed American chestnut that had previously served as rafters in barns; all of the family's objects and books found their ideal place. In this room, a painting by the Japanese artist Kazuo Shiraga hangs above the fireplace. In his paintings and performances, Shiraga materialized his connectedness with whatever materials he was working with; he painted with his feet as his body danced over or was suspended above the canvas. This is a very calm and connected home, an inspiring place to connect to yourself, to nature, and to the universe. Experience the light. Enjoy the views. The seasons change and nature sings "Stay."

PAGE 230
Ascending toward the light,
this secondary staircase designed
by Cutler Anderson Architects
extends from the ground floor to the
main floor of the home. The walls
are painted with whitewash to create
a sense of peace with a quality
of earthiness, underscoring the home's
connection with nature.

LEFT
The presence of nature can be
profoundly felt in this vast room.
The view of Long Island Sound reveals
the three elements of air, light, and
water. Although artfully painted, the
walls have been purposefully left bare
to allow one to enjoy the true art—the
view. In addition to a Chinese stool,
the furniture includes an Axel
Vervoordt Company sofa, club chairs,
and a coffee table made from large,
reclaimed poplar boards which
can be transformed into a dinner table.

PAGE 234

The texture and energy of stones are evident in this view that extends to the media and pool room. Against the far wall is a sculpture by Belgian artist Dominique Stroobant titled *Inter-rompre* (Inter-rupt, 1966). The circle of light is a skylight cut into the terrace above.

PAGE 235

Light streams through a square skylight in the roof onto an oval pane set in the floor of the hall. On top of an eighteenth-century Pyrenean pine table is an earthenware vase by Japanese potter and artist Shiro Tsujimura. The vase holds a tree branch that had fallen during a storm the previous night.

FACING PAGE

Details of the home (from left to right): a wall made of granite and lime plaster presents a harmony of texture and displays the structure of the home; the long hallway leading to the main drawing room and the ocean views beyond; architecture hardware by H. Theophile and the Axel Vervoordt Company on an oak door; an Italian wooden chest of drawers in the guest bedroom; light has a sculptural quality as it takes shape against the whitewashed walls; the view of a corridor made in stone leading to the cigar room, just as the sun is setting; a view of the main staircase created by Cutler Anderson Architects; light and shadow create a dialogue on an antique paving stone from Italy's Piedmont; the view from the top of the staircase toward the home's entrance.

PAGE 238

The view from the kitchen extends through a window over the central staircase into the library, where a cozy fire creates a glowing ambiance.

PAGE 239

The warm library is made from reclaimed chestnut rafters and displays books, drawings, and objects collected by the family over the years, including an edition of *Superficie Magnetica* by Davide Boriani from 1965. Above the fireplace hangs *Gyotai*, a 1979 oil-on-canvas painting by Kazuo Shiraga, one of the most famous members of the post-war Japanese art movement Gutai. The word Gutai means "concreteness" or "embodiment," and the movement was founded by Jiro Yoshihara. Regarding Shiraga's process of painting with his feet, Yoshihara described it as "a means he developed to synthesize the confrontation between the matter chosen by his personal quality and the dynamism in his own mind, in an extremely positive way."

FACING PAGE

Light and shadow interact on a poplar dining table in the main drawing room. The tabletop is supported by trestles, so the table can be moved onto the terrace for dining alfresco. The folding chairs, with linen slipcovers, are by the Axel Vervoordt Company, and on the table is a collection of earthenware by Shiro Tsujimura.

PAGES 242–43

Emanating a sense of peace and tranquility, this view of the main room reveals the magic and power of nature in the surrounding landscape. The elements are ageless and the home forms part of nature. The collection of Axel Vervoordt Company furniture offers a sense of comfort with natural textures. Flexibility is the key, as even the coffee table may be used as a dining table, and the trestle tables can be moved indoors or out to adapt to various occasions. On the right, on top of the round table, is a sculpture by Shiro Tsujimura.

Architecture is the learned game,
correct and magnificent, of forms assembled in the light.
Le Corbusier (1887–1965)

The Albert Canal—which runs some seventy-eight miles (nearly 125 km) from Liege to Antwerp and was named after King Albert I—was created in the 1930s and marked the revival of a nineteenth-century industrial site located along the water's edge, about fifteen minutes from the historic center of Antwerp. Originally founded in 1857, and once the home of Europe's largest distillery, and subsequently a malting complex complete with towering grain silos, this location is remarkable due to its setting and the quality of its buildings, which resides in their authenticity and intrinsic respect for the value of aesthetic and architectural proportions. This series of structures—known simply as Kanaal—now serves as the home for the Axel Vervoordt Company and a specialized staff of nearly one hundred people. Although the company has grown significantly since Axel and May founded it together, following the renovation of the Vlaeykensgang in Antwerp, the guiding philosophies have remained true from the start: share the value of living with art; search for harmony between the past, present, and future; respect timeless objects and reveal their intrinsic value; uncover the beauty of simplicity; embrace authenticity in all that you do. With a seemingly endless supply of energy and creativity, Axel and May continue to inspire and mentor the company, in all of its activities, in the pursuit of this vision. They lead the actions of the Axel and May Vervoordt Foundation and Inspiratum, a group dedicated to the appreciation of music and artistic patronage. Additionally, for the past several years Axel has curated a series of art exhibitions held in various cities and locations, including the Palazzo Fortuny in Venice. Their sons, Boris and Dick, lead the company's day-to-day activities, including the interior design, real estate, home collection, gallery, and art & antiques divisions. Although participation in antique, interior design, and modern and contemporary art fairs, as well as client projects, take the team all over the world, the Kanaal is the hub of company life. In these light-filled offices showcasing art, objects, and furniture, the staff members are deeply invested in their areas of expertise, including interior architecture, archaeology, modern and contemporary art, craftsmanship, product design, restoration, and the supporting roles that make each endeavor possible. The Kanaal is also the future home of the Kanaal Project, an ambitious plan to create nearly one hundred homes and share this unique place with a community of residents. Conceived by the Vervoordt family and created in collaboration with a team that includes Bogdan & Van Broeck Architects, Coussée & Goris Architects, Stéphane Beel Architects, and landscape architect Michel Desvigne, the project's aim is to develop a city in the heart of the country, complete with essential support facilities and businesses, and the future museum for the Axel and May Vervoordt Foundation's collection. Surrounded by art, the philosophy of life here embraces the site's existing architecture and the surrounding elements of nature. A testament to the past, the project reveals a profound respect for the present and offers a comprehensive view on life for the twenty-first century.

PAGE 244
On the third floor of the Kanaal offices,
this light-filled room is used by a team
of art historians to study objects
that span centuries and civilizations,
surrounded by artifacts housed in
a wooden Korean library designed
by Axel Vervoordt. On the table sits
a stone U-shaped yoke (Pre-Columbian,
Early Classic Veracruz culture,
100–600 CE). Dense, highly polished
stone yokes were used as molds for
shaping the protective leather waist
belts worn by ball game players
in contests with spiritual significance.
Hanging against the back wall is
a 1990 gunpowder-on-paper work
by New York-based Chinese artist
Cai Guo-Qiang, titled *Indication (6)—
Project for E.T NO.5.* In front of Qiang's
work is a nineteenth-century Aboriginal
staff. On the shelf below is a wooden
buffalo door used in funerary rites
(Indonesia, Toraja culture, nineteenth
century). On a top shelf at the back
is an Egyptian mummy mask, originally
part of an anthropoid sarcophagus
(Late Period, XXVIth–XXXIst Dynasty,
664–332 BCE).

RIGHT
In the loft sitting room overlooking
the canal is a selection of furniture,
art, and objects, including sofas
and chairs from the Axel Vervoordt
Home Collection. On the back wall,
on the right, is *Work I* (1963) by
Japanese Gutai artist Norio Imai.
On the left is *Lateral Swelling* (1963)
by Japanese artist Tsuyoshi Maekawa.
In the background is a wood and
bronze conference table designed
by Jules Wabbes in 1972, upon which
rest large Egyptian alabaster vessels.
Also in the background, on the right,
is a sculpture by Athena Poilâne.
In the middle ground is a 1953
rounded-back armchair made
of oak, fabric, and leather by Danish
designer Hans Wegner (1914–2007),
and a 1953 leather armchair by Danish
designer Erik Kolling Andersen.
On the coffee table rests a pair
of Egyptian handled vases from
the early Dynastic and Pre-Dynastic
periods, along with a fossilized
mammoth molar. In the foreground
is a sculpture made of branches
and twigs in 2010 by the Dutch
artist Sjoerd Buisman.

PAGE 248

On the third floor of Kanaal, light softly drapes a pair of ornamental funerary turbans sculpted in marble, from the Ottoman Empire (Turkey, eighteenth–nineteenth century). Both are presented on antique artist's stands. On the wall hangs an untitled 1968 pencil-on-paper work by the Dutch artist Armando.

PAGE 249

Light, shadow, electricity, and form are all present in this corner of a whitewashed gallery space. Eileen Gray designed the tubular iron garden stool in 1929 for the E1207 Villa in Roquebrune, in southern France. The chair sits next to a gelatin silver print titled "Lightning Fields 236" by Hiroshi Sugimoto. Describing this type of work, the artist commented, "The idea of observing the effects of electrical discharges on photographic dry plates reflects my desire to re-create the major discoveries of these scientific pioneers in the darkroom, and verify them with my own eyes."

FACING PAGE

Details of the offices (clockwise from top left): a sharpened pencil in the company's workshop reflects a commitment to pure art and design; a view of the working table in the fabric department during a collaborative client meeting; rolls of Belgian linen; a view of the staff office is a testimony to the team's passion for working closely together, sharing knowledge, and communicating.

PAGE 252

Working tables are always available for meetings with colleagues and guests. Light shines across the table, illuminating a scale model for a project in Russia, and reflects the historic character of the site and the dreams of its future residents.

PAGE 253

A wall of samples demonstrates the diversity of textures and materials that are often developed for specific projects, and some are also kept in stock.

LEFT
Like sculptures rising out of the ground toward the sky, these industrial silos at the Kanaal site will be transformed into new apartments. This image shows the work in progress. The team of architects comprises Bogdan & Van Broeck Architects, Coussée & Goris Architects, Stéphane Beel Architects BVBA, and landscape architect Michel Desvigne.

PAGE 256
A sketch for a project by architect Stéphane Beel.

PAGE 257
An upward view of two of the site's landmarks: the silos and the tower.

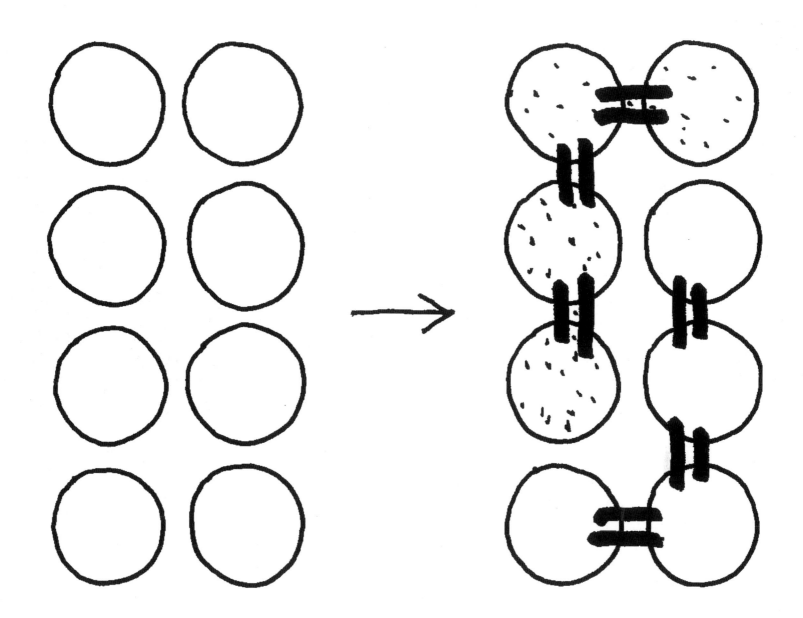

Thank you for the light.

We would like to express our deepest gratitude to every person who has put their heart and effort into creating these dream homes. In the process, they've helped create and share happiness and warmth with the owners and their families and friends.

With a lifetime of respect and gratitude, we would like to thank our clients and their families for allowing us to be part of their personal stories and for sharing these experiences with us. We're endlessly inspired by your vision and friendship.

Thank you to our team of collaborators—without whom we could never work on such international projects concurrently—for their intelligence and dedication. The timeless search for harmony cannot be simply duplicated; it takes us on a path that needs to be discovered with every new project, as we seek to grasp the essence of the place the project occupies. Through their skill, experience, and knowledge, our collaborators are not only able to consistently reinvent themselves, but are also able to translate the vision of the company and its founders—Axel and May—and form the essential link to build and strengthen relationships with the families for whom we create these homes.

Thank you to Laziz Hamani, whose incomparable vision behind the lens is able to capture light in such an essential way that we can feel it on our skin. We admire your talent and appreciate your friendship.

Thank you to Michael Gardner for writing such captivating texts and structuring the book with the help of wise quotes that frame the elements of our philosophy. Through your words, you've been able to convey exactly how each home feels.

Thank you to Ghislaine Bavoillot and her entire team at Flammarion for managing every detail of this project and allowing the creative force of the book to express itself. It feels, as always, very natural to work together, and we thank you for sharing the experience with us for the fourth time.

Thank you to all of our collaborators at the Axel Vervoordt Company, who make everything possible: Ali Zaryouh, Anke Van Camp, Ann De Pessemier, Ann Van den Broeck, Anne De Clercq, Annelies Castelein, Anne-Sophie Dusselier, Arben Osman, Barbara De Belder, Bjorn Schrevens, Bram Van Scharen, Ceryl Locht, Chris De Pauw, Christophe Verhoeven, Dave Wene, David De Schryver, Diana Banach, Didier Ullens de Schooten, Dirk De Belder, Dirk Herman, Dirk Van der Kerken, Ellen Van Quickelberghe, Els Dandois, Erik Van der Pas, Evy De Meersman, Francis Joris, François Van Schevensteen, Frank Van Putte, Giuseppe Allegra, Goedele Vets, Goedele Zwaenepoel, Hilda De Lie, Hilde Van de Veire, Iris Clemens, Jan Smets, Jason Collins, Jef Sips, Jenke Van den Akkerveken, Jim Corbett, Jitti Rattanabute, Johan De Pooter, Johannes Roeder, Joris Mampaey, Jose Van Haaster, Julie Denkens, Jurgen Verdyck, Karolien Liekens, Katrien Dehandschutter, Katrijn Prosec, Koen De Kock, Koen Van den Bussche, Kris Rosenfeld, Leslaw Zablotny, Lieven Anseeuw, Lieven Winkels, Liselotte Vernieuwe, Luc Joossens, Marc Pollentier, Marie-Christine Moeris, Mario Bruyneel, Mark Laenen, Michael Schoremens, Michael Severs, Mieke Vanderschoot, Nasica Benali, Nathalie Reyns, Nick Peeters, Nico Goethals, Nikki Konings, Noach Vander Beken, Pascale Van Aertselaer, Patrick Vermeulen, Philip Feyfer, Robert Lauwers, Sara Segers, Sarah Roux, Silvan Vandaele, Sue Vanschoubroeck, Thekla De Leeuw, Tine Anseeuw, Tom Bovyn, Tom Geluykens, Veerle Pauwels, Veerle Van Sande, Vera De Nijs, Walter Van de Venne, Wilfried De Raedt, Wilfried en Lieve Vergotte, William Schenk, Wim Dumarey, Wim Pues, Wolf Schelkens, Yannick Van Schevensteen.

Boris Vervoordt

Writing is the geometry of the soul.
Plato (c. 428/427–348/347 BCE)

A mentor once told me that one of the pleasures of books is that they satisfy one of our fundamental curiosities: "We read in order to find out how other people think." I believe that. I also believe that a very similar logic applies to the beauty of a book like this one. Driven by a cautious curiosity, we review these pages with a desire to learn how an interior designer thinks, and to enter the private lives of others to see how they live. It's a window into the minds and lives of others, with the purpose of sharing experiences, knowledge, and light.

Through their willingness to share their private worlds, the owners of these homes have expressed courage and generosity, for which we should be enormously grateful, and I am. Thank you.

For guiding me through the projects and process, and providing their direct insight and research, I'm thankful to Barbara de Belder, Erik Van der Pas, Philip Feyfer, Goedele Zwaenepoel, Veerle Pauwels, and everyone who made a contribution behind the scenes. For their time, attention to detail, and enormous efforts in the complexities of every endeavor, thank you to the team at the Axel Vervoordt Company. I'm grateful to have learned so much with their help.

With their creativity and skill at revealing the light, Laziz and Antoine help us to see what we otherwise would not. I am very thankful and humbled by their talent.

For their exceptional guidance, experience, and leadership, I wish to thank Ghislaine, Flavie, Kate, Isabelle, and their team at Flammarion. Thank you very much for including me.

And thanks to Axel, May, Dick, and Boris, for all of their endless gifts—the most important being the act of sharing. In doing so, the spirit of their generosity is felt by many. The art of living is renewed daily. We are so lucky. I thank them with all of my heart.

In search of vision, we looked to the sea.
In search of inspiration, we studied the elements of nature.
In search of renewal, we turned toward the light.
In search of oneself, we yearned for home.

Michael Gardner

FACING PAGE
As seen from the silos, a flock of birds sweeps across the sky as the sun sets over the water, in a view from Kanaal toward the city of Antwerp.

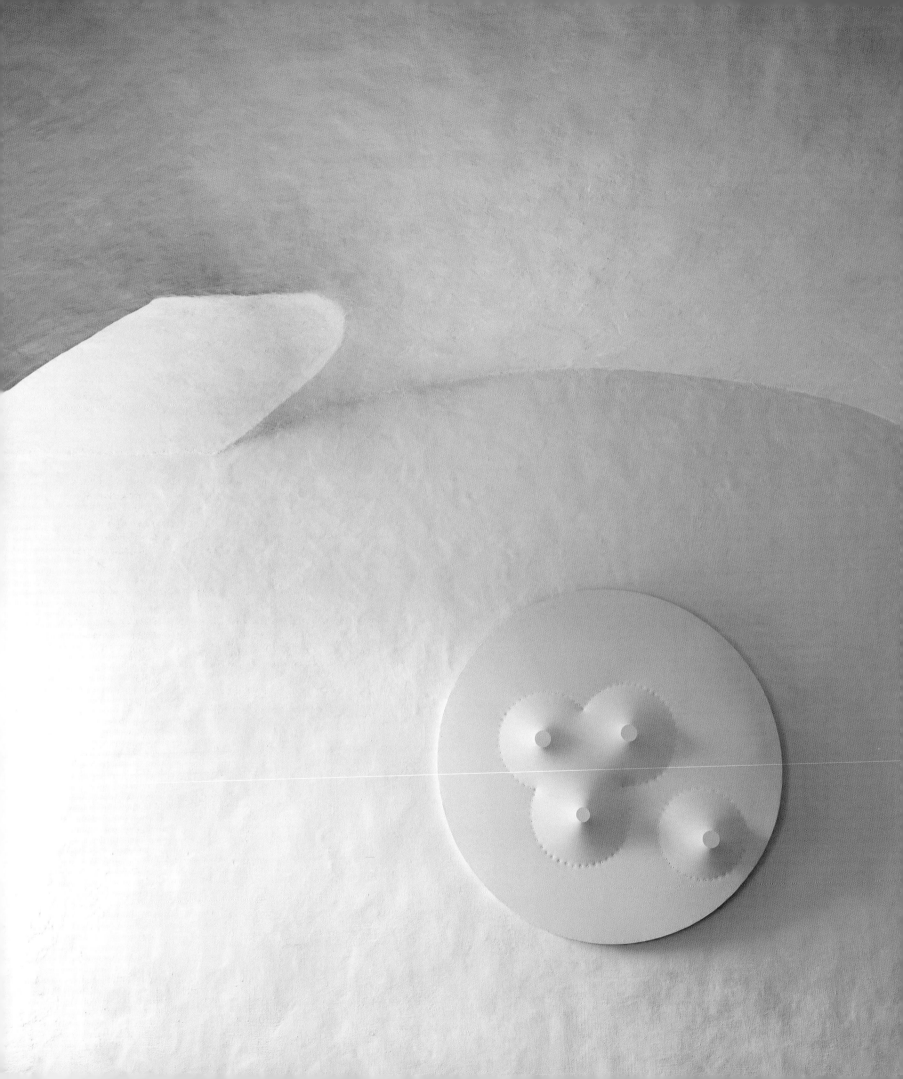

I dedicate this book to my friend Axel Vervoodt.

In life, there are those who let their light shine, who share their passion for living, who follow their dreams. There are those who teach you to open your eyes and really see, and invite you into a more human, more truthful world. There are those who show you how to discover yourself, and wake you from the long sleep that life has plunged you into. Axel is all of these people. I remember that day in September when he called me just as I was at the edge of an abyss, when it seemed as if there was nothing left. I can still remember his exact words: "Are you free at the moment? I would like you to photograph a house, because you are the only one who can understand it, I need your eye." On that day, he offered me one of the best gifts of my life. Illness had me in its clutches and I had no energy left, everything seemed beyond my reach, everything had faded and vanished, until the moment I entered that magical yet crazy place.

Axel, your joy, your light, your spirit awoke in me a force that I thought had disappeared forever. I rediscovered my love for life, for my passion; I picked up my camera again and could finally see the world opening up for me once more.

Thank you, Axel, for your generosity, for your breath of life. I still remember the name of that house which bore the word "Vie" (life). Sometimes, things are not mere coincidences. We never tell our friends enough how much we love them. Axel, you are my eternal friend and I thank you.

I can remember perfectly the day we decided to create this book; one of the most important moments in this adventure, and it all started on a boat. Apollonia, Boris, Michael, and I were drawing up to a little island off the coast of Brittany. There was a constant wind, the light broke through the clouds with incredible force, there was a constant array of changing colors, and the sea accentuated the sun's powerful rays, the water acting as a mirror to the sky. The evanescence of the rays illuminated the island in quite a different way. Then, as we disembarked onto the island, all my doubts magically disappeared; there was a poetic force that seemed to benevolently welcome me in.

Throughout this adventure, I was guided by Boris Vervoordt, and together we produced images of all these places bathed in light, where sometimes the world seemed to stand still. Each of these houses was in a state of perfect harmony with the surrounding nature. Each one had a soul, held secrets, but still generously opened its doors to us. This book was created in spaces that are unique, timeless; spaces where dreams come alive.

Firstly, I wish to thank those who opened up their homes to us with such generosity and simplicity. Without them, there could have been no images.

Thank you:
To Boris Vervoordt, for letting me experience a new adventure, and, above all, for entrusting me with this book.
To Antoine Lippens, my assistant, who worked diligently throughout this project to bring all of these images into existence.
To Digitline Studio, Romuald Habert, Pascal Gillet, Matthieu Chestier, for their work on the lighting and editing of the photographs.
To Yohann Gendry for his help, and the pleasure of working with him again in London.
To Lucien Audibert, my second assistant, for managing the images.
To Ghislaine Bavoillot, for her generous presence and contribution to the construction of this book.
To Isabelle Ducat, the artistic director, for assembling these images in such a way that they might come alive together.
To my sons—Yannis, Mathis, and Noham—who I love, and who accompany me everywhere and pass their innocent, joyful energy on to me every day.
And finally to all those who have contributed to the making of this book.
Thank you all.

Laziz Hamani

FACING PAGE
Work–Circle B (1964) by Norio Imai
hangs in the cellar of s'Gravenwezel castle.

Photographic Credits

p. 4 © Gotthard Graubner, © Shiro Tsujimura

p. 8 © Jef Verheyen / ADAGP 2013

p. 10 © Antoni Tàpies / ADAGP 2013, © Shiro Tsujimura *Slash Dish*, © Karl Prantl / ADAGP 2013 *Stein zur Meditation*

pp. 18–19 © Jef Verheyen / ADAGP 2013, © Pierre Jeanneret / ADAGP 2013, © Michel Mouffe

p. 21 © Jef Verheyen / ADAGP 2013, © Sadaharu Horio

p. 22 © Pierre Jeanneret / ADAGP 2013

p. 27 © Hans van der Laan / ADAGP 2013 *Monastery Bench*, © Günther Uecker / ADAGP 2013 *Regen*

p. 33 © Antoni Tàpies / ADAGP 2013 *Composition with Brown Matter*

p. 36 © Raimund Girke / ADAGP 2013, © Antoine Mortier / ADAGP 2013, © Henri Michaux / ADAGP 2013

pp. 38–39 © Davide Boriani, © Antoni Tàpies / ADAGP 2013, © Heinz Mack / ADAGP 2013, © Jean Arp / ADAGP 2013

p. 41 Antoni Tàpies / ADAGP 2013, © Jean Arp / ADAGP 2013

p. 42 © Gotthard Graubner *Stilles Leuchten II*

pp. 44–45 © Antoni Tàpies / ADAGP 2013, © Hans Hartung / ADAGP 2013, © Pierre Jeanneret / ADAGP 2013

p. 49 © Gotthard Graubner (bottom left, detail)

p. 51 © Roman Opalka / ADAGP 2013

pp. 52, 54–55, 56–57 © Günther Uecker / ADAGP 2013 *Interferenzen*, © Serge Poliakoff / ADAGP 2013, © Lucio Fontana / ADAGP 2013 *Attese*, © Dominique Stroobant

p. 58 © Kazuo Shiraga

p. 61 © Piero Manzoni / ADAGP 2013

p. 67 © Shiro Tsujimura, © Lucio Fontana / ADAGP 2013

p. 76 © Jef Verheyen / ADAGP 2013 *Paar – Lichstroom*

pp. 80–81 © Marc Chagall / ADAGP 2013 *L'Âne Rouge*

p. 88 © Anish Kapoor / ADAGP 2013

p. 91 © Ellsworth Kelly

pp. 92–93 © William Turnbull / ADAGP 2013, © Joel Shapiro / ADAGP 2013, © Markus Raetz / ADAGP 2013

pp. 96–97, 98 © Enrico Castellani / ADAGP 2013 *Senza Titolo*

p. 103 © Markus Raetz / ADAGP 2013

pp. 104–5 © Herbert Brandl *Weidenmulde*

p. 124 © Sandra Zeenni *Bouteilles blanches*, © Kees Goudzwaard, © Michel François / ADAGP 2013, © Nadia Pasquer *Polyèdres*

pp. 126–27 © Pat Steir *Waterfall*, © Le Corbusier / ADAGP 2013

p. 129 © Sadaharu Horio, © Jeff Koons, © Michel François / ADAGP 2013, © Keith Haring, © Kees Goudzwaard, © Jean Prouvé

p. 132 © Serge Mouille / ADAGP 2013, © Richard Serra / ADAGP 2013

p. 133 © Tony Cragg / ADAGP 2013

pp. 134–35 © El Anatsui *A Stitch in Time, II* © Jules Wabbes / ADAGP 2013

p. 139 © Jules Wabbes / ADAGP 2013

p. 144 © Charlotte Perriand / ADAGP 2013

p. 147 © Annick Tapernoux, © Pierre Jeanneret / ADAGP 2013

p. 149 © Annick Tapernoux, © Pierre Jeanneret / ADAGP 2013, © Yves Klein / ADAGP 2013

pp. 150–51 © Michel François / ADAGP 2013, © Serge Mouille / ADAGP 2013, © Pierre Jeanneret / ADAGP 2013, © Charlotte Perriand / ADAGP 2013

p. 153 © Dominique Stroobant, © Hiroshi Sugimoto

p. 154 © Anish Kapoor / ADAGP 2013, © Le Corbusier / ADAGP 2013, © Jean Prouvé *Visiteur*, © Lucio Fontana / ADAGP 2013

p. 155 © Lucio Fontana / ADAGP 2013

p. 156 © Le Corbusier / ADAGP 2013

p. 157 © Jean Prouvé *Visiteur*

pp. 158–59 © Jef Verheyen / ADAGP 2013 *Night and Day*

pp. 160–61 © Nakajima Yasumi, © Jean Perzel / ADAGP 2013, © Jean-Michel Frank

p. 162 © Günther Uecker / ADAGP 2013, © Shozo Shimamoto

pp. 164–65 © Shiro Tsujimura, © Kazuo Shiraga

p. 166 © Kazuo Shiraga

p. 167 © Günther Uecker / ADAGP 2013

p. 175 © Sadaharu Horio *Atarimae-no-koto*

pp. 180–81 © Massimo Micheluzzi, © Jef Verheyen / ADAGP 2013, © Nadia Pasquer, © Jules Wabbes / ADAGP 2013, © Jean Girel / ADAGP 2013

pp. 182–83 © Enrico Castellani / ADAGP 2013

p. 185 © Massimo Micheluzzi, © Nadia Pasquer, © Walter Leblanc / ADAGP 2013 *Twisted Strings, Phase I – II –III*

pp. 188–89 © Jean Girel / ADAGP 2013

p. 193 © Dirk Vander Eecken *The Door of Invisibility*

p. 195 © Dirk Vander Eecken *Fault ovale*

p. 198 © Anish Kapoor / ADAGP 2013

p. 208 © Vilhelm Lauritzen, © Paul Dupré-Lafon / ADAGP 2013

p. 210 © Pierre Jeanneret / ADAGP 2013

p. 211 © Günther Uecker / ADAGP 2013 *Haar der Nymphen*

p. 213 © Dominique Stroobant, © Pierre Jeanneret / ADAGP 2013

p. 215 © Adam Fuss, © Carlo Zauli, © Jules Wabbes / ADAGP 2013, © Serge Mouille / ADAGP 2013

pp. 216–17 © Le Corbusier / ADAGP 2013 *Long Island*

p. 218 © Ed Ruscha *Clock*, © Anselm Kiefer, © Fondation Picasso *Verre et Bouteille de Bass sur une Table*, © Ben Nicholson / ADAGP 2013, © Richard Serra / ADAGP 2013 *Canadian Pacific*

pp. 220–21 © Adam Fuss *Details of Love*, © Jean Dubuffet / ADAGP 2013 *The Deviant*, © Hans Hofmann, © Succession Giacometti (Fondation Alberto & Annette Giacometti, Paris + ADAGP 2013) Alberto Giacometti, *Diego au Manteau*, 1954, Bronze 15 x 13 ½ x 8 ¾ in. (38.1 x 34.5 x 22.3 cm), 2/6, cast 1959, Susse Fondeur foundry, private collection, New York. AGD 1847

p. 222 © Jean Dubuffet / ADAGP 2013 *Barbe de Voyance*

p. 223 © Anselm Kiefer *Leonardo Pisano*, © James Welling *#14* © Jules Wabbes / ADAGP 2013

p. 225 © Joan Miró / ADAGP 2013

pp. 226–27 © Ed Ruscha *Words Going Round #3*, © Helen Frankenthaler / ADAGP 2013

p. 228 © Arnold Newman

p. 229 © Adam Fuss © Hiroshi Sugimoto

p. 234 © Dominique Stroobant

p. 235 © Shiro Tsujimura

p. 237 © Jean-Édouard Vuillard

p. 238–39 © Kazuo Shiraga *Gyotai*

pp. 246–47 © Tsuyoshi Maekawa *Lateral Swelling*, © Norio Imai, © Jules Wabbes / ADAGP 2013, © Sjoerd Buisman, © Erik Kolling Andersen

p. 248 © Armando

p. 249 © Hiroshi Sugimoto *Lightning Fields 236*

p. 260 © Norio Imai *Work–Circle B*

Editorial Director: Ghislaine Bavoillot
Design and Typesetting: Isabelle Ducat
Copyediting: Judith Fayard
Proofreading: Helen Downey
Color Separation: IGS, L'Isle d'Espagnac, France
Printed in Italy by Grafiche Flaminia

Simultaneously published
in French as *Maisons de Lumière*
© Flammarion, S.A., Paris, 2013

English-language edition
© Flammarion, S.A., Paris, 2013

13 14 15 3 2 1

ISBN: 978-2-08-020159-1

Dépôt légal: 10/2013

"Shadows are all we have to
show us the shapes that light can make."
—Adam Gopnik